MAKE,
BAKE,
CUPCAKE
the recipe book

MAKE, BAKE, CUPCAKE
the recipe book

BORED BAKERS REJOICE — THE CUPCAKE REVOLUTION IS HERE!

LOVE FOOD™

CONTENTS

Baked To Perfection

What's not to love? Cupcakes are sinfully decadent, but inherently portion controlled; delightfully whimsical, but with a welcome air of simplicity. Since they're made in individual servings, there's no need to hassle with cutting and serving and there's never a tussle over the corner piece, since each and every one delivers the perfect ratio of frosting to cake.

Once baked, cupcakes become a blank canvas on which you can create your own artistic masterpieces. Using various types of frosting, sprinkles, decorating sugars and fondant forms, you can make a cupcake that looks like just about anything.

No matter what flavour cakes you choose or how you decide to adorn them, making delicious cupcakes is a breeze and decorating them is much easier than you might imagine. Just follow our simple tips and you'll be baking up your own decadent, adorable little cups of cake in no time.

Once you've mastered the recipes and techniques, you'll be able to create cupcakes to suit just about any occasion. Happy baking, decorating and, of course, devouring!

Recipe basics

Certain terms crop up time and time again within the cupcake recipes that follow – so familiarize yourself with the basics below before proceeding with your very own cupcake revolution!

Eggs and sugar

Beating together eggs and sugar may seem like a no-brainer, but it's important to cream the butter and sugar together before adding further ingredients, to prevent curdling. To create a pale and fluffy mixture, beat for 3–5 minutes using an electric mixer set on medium speed.

Adding eggs

Always add eggs one at a time to the butter and sugar. There is no need to pre-beat the eggs, simply beat the mixture after the addition of each egg until it is fully incorporated.

Mixing flour

Once the flour has been added, you should only mix as long as is necessary to fully incorporate. It's important to scrape down the bottom and sides of the mixing bowl frequently between additions to ensure that all the ingredients are well mixed.

Filling cases

Once mixed, scoop the batter into the paper-lined cupcake tin. Fill each cup about two-thirds full – just the right amount to produce a nice, dome-shaped cupcake that will prove the perfect base for decorating. Unless otherwise specified in the recipe, divide the cupcake batter equally between the prepared cupcake cases.

Oven baking

To avoid overcooking, test the cupcakes 1–2 minutes before the recommended cooking time is up. Insert a skewer into the centre of a cupcake – if properly baked, it should come out clean.

Cooling cupcakes

When the cupcakes are risen and cooked through, remove from the oven promptly and let them cool in the tin for 1–2 minutes, until they are cool enough to handle. Using a spatula or small knife, lift the cupcakes (in their paper cases) from the tin and transfer them to a wire rack to cool completely.

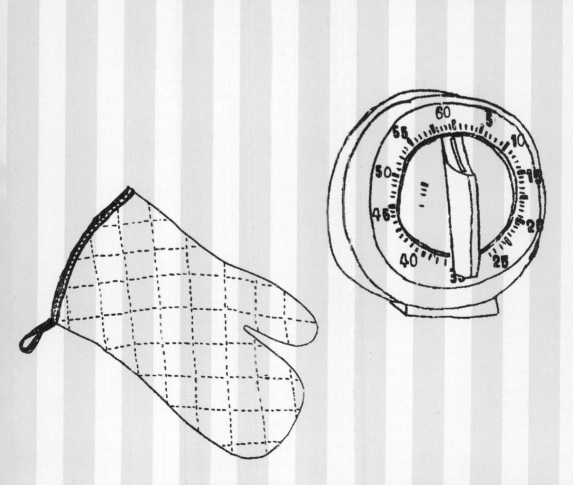

The Icing On The Cake

Frosting, generally speaking, is a fluffy, sugary icing used for topping cakes and cupcakes. Although this is a blanket term, there are various different types, and each is suitable for a different finish.

Basic buttercream

Made from butter and icing sugar, usually with a bit of milk added along with plant extracts, cocoa powder, citrus juice or other flavourings. Buttercream frosting can be spread with a palette knife or piped onto cupcakes with any number of decorative tips. It is simple to make and holds its shape well, making it an easy topping for decorating cupcakes.

Cooked buttercream

Also sometimes called Swiss buttercream, this is made from sugar, butter and whipped egg whites – it is lighter and less sweet than basic buttercream, as it gets its structure from the egg whites, not the volume of icing sugar used. It is a bit more laborious to make than regular buttercream since the egg whites have to be heated (the sugar is dissolved in the egg whites as they heat) and then whipped to stiff peaks before the butter is added, but the result is a more refined frosting that is excellent for spreading or piping and, like basic buttercream, holds its shape well. A stand mixer is highly recommended for making this type of frosting, but a hand-held electric mixer will work, too.

Cream cheese frosting

Cream cheese frosting is similar to a basic buttercream, but some of the butter is replaced with cream cheese for a lighter texture and a less sweet flavour.

Meringue frosting

Meringue frostings is lighter than either type of buttercream, since it consists primarily of egg whites and sugar, with no added fat. Cream of tartar, a stabilizer, is often used to add stiffness to meringue frostings. It is ideal for piping into etherial, fluffy swirls, but is best eaten on the day of making. Again, a stand mixer is highly recommended for making meringue frosting, but a hand-held electric mixer will work as well.

Fondant

Fondant is the stiff, rolled icing that often adorns wedding cakes. The appeal of fondant is that it has a texture similar to a stiff play dough and can be coloured, rolled, cut, molded and shaped into all sorts of designs, and gives a polished look to your confections. Some people don't like the taste of fondant, though it can be flavoured using concentrated flavouring oils or extracts.

You needn't go to the trouble of making your own fondant since ready-to-roll fondant, both white, ready to be coloured to your liking – or pre-coloured, is available at most supermarkets. To colour fondant yourself, use gel or paste colouring to achieve vibrant hues without affecting the consistency with too much liquid.

Ganache

Ganache is a rich, creamy frosting made by melting chocolate with cream. It can be used as a glossy glaze, poured while it is still warm, or a filling that thickens to a truffle-like consistency as it cools. Ganache is a snap to make. Simply combine the chocolate and cream, in a heatproof bowl set over simmering water, until the chocolate is almost melted. Stir until the chocolate is completely melted and the cream is fully incorporated.

Piping Perfection

To fill a piping bag, cut off about 1 cm/½ inch from the tip and insert your piping tip. Fold the sides down over your hand (alternatively, you can place the bag in a tall glass or jug, folding the bag down over the sides) and, using the other hand, scoop the frosting in using a rubber spatula. Fill the piping bag about two-thirds full. Remove any air pockets, close up the bag at the top, and seal with a twist tie.

To pipe swirls, use a pastry bag fitted with a star-shaped or round tip. Begin piping at the outer edge, holding the tip straight up and down, about 1 cm/½ inch above the top of the cupcake, and gently squeeze the bag from the top. Work your way around the cupcake in an outside-in spiral. When you reach the centre, stop squeezing and gently pull the tip straight up and away from the top of the cupcake.

You can also use a star-shaped tip to cover the top of the cupcake with individual frosting stars. Simply hold the filled bag, fitted with a star-shaped tip over the top of the cupcake, squeeze a bit of frosting out onto the cake, stop squeezing and pull the bag straight up away from the cake. Repeat until the entire top of the cake is covered.

Essential decorating equipment

• Pastry bags, either disposable or reusable, coupled with decorative piping tips, are extremely useful for piping frosting to create different effects. You can also use heavy-duty plastic ziplock bags as piping bags by snipping the corner and inserting a piping tip.

• Piping tips come in dozens of shapes and sizes, from tiny star-shaped tips to large round ones and flat ones, and even ones with multiple holes that are perfect for making frosting hair, fur, or grass. You can buy the tips individually or in sets. A basic starter set is all you need for the recipes in this book, but as you get more adventurous, you might want to invest in a larger set.

• An offset spatula is useful for spreading frosting onto cupcakes when you don't want to pipe it. You can buy an offset spatula at any kitchen shop.

All about decorating

Paper cases
Cupcake cases form the visual foundation of your work of art, so choose accordingly. If you choose delicate or light coloured cases, you may want to bake your cupcakes in plain liners and add the decorative ones after cooking so that they remain crisp and clean.

Food colouring
We recommend gel or paste food colourings rather than the liquid type, for more vibrant colours.

Sprinkles
You can buy sprinkles, confetti and decorating sugar in any colour or shape. Spend some time browsing the decorating aisle at your supermarket, craft store or cake decorating supply shop to get ideas.

Fondant decorations
You can buy decorations made by pressing fondant into moulds and then letting it dry until it is hard. These come in just about any shape you can imagine, from skeleton bones to flowers to eyeballs and more.

Writing icing
Sold in tubes in various colours, writing icing is perfect for adding detailed design elements and, of course, for writing words on your cupcakes.

Edible ink markers
Just like the markers you use to draw or colour, but made with edible ink, these come in a wide range of colours and are fantastic for adding detail onto fondant or other firm surfaces.

Chocolate-flavoured cake covering
These bars of chocolate have been tempered to ensure the right texture when melted. They are used to make chocolate coatings with a crisp finish.

Storage & Eating

• Always cool cupcakes completely (30 to 45 minutes) before covering.

• Store unfrosted cupcakes or those with cream cheese or whipped cream based frosting covered in the refrigerator for up to three days.

• Cupcakes frosted with buttercream frosting can be stored, covered, at room temperature for up to three days.

• Cupcakes frosted with meringue frosting should be eaten the day they are made.

• Unfrosted cupcakes can also be frozen, in a single layer in a sealed container, for up to three months. Frost them while they are still frozen, and then defrost them in the refrigerator for several hours. Bring to room temperature before serving.

• Most frostings, too, can be refrigerated or frozen. Buttercream or cream cheese frosting can be stored, in a tightly covered container, in the refrigerator for up to two weeks or in the freezer for up to six months. Thaw frozen frosting in the refrigerator and beat it with an electric mixer for a minute or two before using.

• Ready-to-roll fondant can be stored indefinitely at room temperature, tightly wrapped in clingfilm in a cool, dry place.

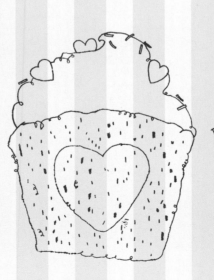

CHAPTER 1
COCKTAILS &
MOCKTAILS

Margarita Cupcakes

makes 12

190 g/6¾ oz plain flour

1½ tsp baking powder

¼ tsp salt

115 g/4 oz unsalted butter, softened

200 g/7 oz caster sugar

2 tsp vanilla extract

2 large eggs

90 ml/3 fl oz milk

3 tbsp tequila

finely grated rind and juice of 1 lime

frosting

3 large egg whites

150 g/5½ oz granulated sugar

225 g/8 oz unsalted butter, softened

4 tbsp triple sec

finely grated rind of 1 lime

green food colouring

1. Preheat the oven to 180°C/350°F/Gas Mark 4 and line a 12-hole cupcake tin with paper cases.

2. Sift together the flour, baking powder and salt in a bowl. Put the butter and caster sugar into a separate bowl and beat until pale and fluffy. Add the vanilla extract and the eggs, one at a time, beating after each addition. Add half of the flour mixture and the milk, tequila and lime rind and juice, and beat until combined. Add the remaining flour mixture and mix.

3. Spoon the batter into the paper cases and bake in the preheated oven for 20 minutes, until risen and golden. Leave to cool in the tin for 1–2 minutes, then transfer to a wire rack to cool completely.

4. To make the frosting, put the egg whites and granulated sugar in a heatproof bowl set over a saucepan of gently simmering water and whisk until the sugar has completely dissolved. Remove from the heat and whisk the mixture for 4–5 minutes. Add the butter, 2 tablespoons at a time, and continue to whisk until it holds stiff peaks. Add the triple sec, lime rind and 2 drops of food colouring and stir until just combined.

5. Spoon the frosting into a piping bag fitted with a star-shaped tip and pipe it onto the cupcakes.

Top tip

Swap the tequila in the batter for
lime juice, and the triple sec in the
frosting for orange juice to make this
non-alcoholic.

Pina Colada Cupcakes

makes 12

190 g/6¾ oz plain flour

1½ tsp baking powder

¼ tsp salt

115 g/4 oz unsalted butter, softened

200 g/7 oz caster sugar

2 large eggs

2 tbsp white rum

125 ml/4 fl oz milk

85 g/3 oz canned pineapple, drained and crushed with a fork

60 g/2¼ oz toasted desiccated coconut

12 cocktail umbrellas, to decorate

frosting

4 large egg whites

200 g/7 oz granulated sugar

¼ tsp cream of tartar

1 tbsp coconut extract

2 tbsp coconut cream

1. Preheat the oven to 180°C/350°F/Gas Mark 4 and line a 12-hole cupcake tin with paper cases.

2. Sift together the flour, baking powder and salt in a bowl. Put the butter and caster sugar into a separate bowl and beat until pale and fluffy. Add the eggs, one at a time, beating after each addition. Add the rum, milk and half of the flour mixture, and beat until combined. Add the remaining flour mixture and mix. Stir in the pineapple.

3. Spoon the batter into the paper cases and bake in the preheated oven for 20 minutes, until risen and golden. Leave to cool in the tin for 1–2 minutes, then transfer to a wire rack to cool completely.

4. To make the frosting, put the egg whites, granulated sugar and cream of tartar in a heatproof bowl set over a saucepan of gently simmering water and whisk until the sugar has completely dissolved. Remove from the heat and whisk the mixture for 4–5 minutes or until it holds stiff peaks. Add the coconut extract and coconut cream and stir until just combined. Spoon the frosting into a piping bag fitted with a star-shaped tip and pipe onto the cupcakes.

5. Sprinkle with toasted desiccated coconut and decorate each cupcake with a cocktail umbrella.

Cosmopolitan Cupcakes

makes 12

190 g/6¾ oz plain flour

1½ tsp baking powder

¼ tsp salt

115 g/4 oz unsalted butter, softened

200 g/7 oz caster sugar

1 tsp vanilla extract

2 large eggs

1 tbsp lime juice

1 tsp finely grated lime rind

2 tbsp cranberry-flavoured vodka

1 tbsp triple sec

4 tbsp milk

pink food colouring

frosting

115 g/4 oz unsalted butter, softened

about 250 g/9 oz icing sugar (see method)

2 tbsp cranberry-flavoured vodka

1 tsp vanilla extract

pink food colouring

to decorate

pink sugar crystals

115 g/4 oz marzipan

green food colouring

black edible-ink marker

12 cocktail umbrellas

1. Preheat the oven to 180°C/350°F/Gas Mark 4. Line a 12-hole cupcake tin with paper cases.

2. Sift together the flour, baking powder and salt in a bowl. Put the butter and caster sugar into a separate bowl and beat until pale and fluffy. Add the vanilla extract, then add the eggs, one at a time, beating after each addition. Add the lime juice, lime rind, vodka, triple sec, milk and half of the flour mixture and beat until combined. Add the remaining flour mixture and mix. Stir in a few drops of food colouring and beat until evenly incorporated.

3. Spoon the batter into the paper cases and bake in the preheated oven for 20 minutes, until risen and a cocktail stick inserted into the centre of a cupcake comes out clean. Leave to cool in the tin for 1–2 minutes, then transfer to a wire rack to cool completely.

4. To make the frosting, put the butter into a bowl and beat with an electric mixer until pale and creamy. Add the icing sugar along with the vodka and vanilla extract. Beat together until well combined. Add more icing sugar, if necessary, to achieve a piping consistency. Add a few drops of food colouring and mix until evenly incorporated.

5. Spoon the frosting into a piping bag fitted with a star-shaped tip. Pipe the frosting onto the cupcakes and sprinkle with the pink sugar crystals, to decorate.

6. To make the lime wedge decorations, divide the marzipan in half. Add a few drops of green food colouring to one half and knead until evenly incorporated. Add more colour if needed to achieve a dark green colour – this will be used to make the lime rind. Add a couple of drops of green food colouring to the remaining piece of marzipan and knead until evenly incorporated – this will be used to make the inside of the lime wedge, so it should be light green in colour.

7. Divide both marzipan colours into 12 pieces. Take one piece of light green marzipan and shape into a semi-circle about 5 mm/¼ inch thick. Lightly pinch the flat side of the semi-circle to make a wedge shape. Flatten a piece of the dark green marzipan and press in place around the curved edge of the wedge, trimming as necessary to give the effect of a rind. Repeat with the remaining marzipan to make 12 lime wedges in total. Using the edible-ink marker, draw lines on the lighter green part to represent the inner membrane of a lime wedge. Set aside to dry.

8. To serve, place a lime wedge on top of each cupcake and insert a cocktail umbrella.

5

6

8

Top tip

To make a boozeless batter, swap the cranberry-flavoured vodka for cranberry juice and the triple sec for orange juice. The vodka in the frosting can also be swapped for cranberry juice.

Mudslide Cupcakes

makes 12

125 g/4½ oz plain flour

60 g/2¼ oz cocoa powder

1½ tsp baking powder

¼ tsp salt

115 g/4 oz unsalted butter, softened

200 g/7 oz caster sugar

2 tsp vanilla extract

2 large eggs

125 ml/4 fl oz double cream

40 g/1½ oz plain chocolate chips, plus extra for decorating

frosting

60 g/2¼ oz unsalted butter, softened

about 250 g/9 oz icing sugar (see method)

2 tbsp milk

3 tbsp Irish cream liqueur

1 tsp vanilla extract

chocolate sauce

55 g/2 oz plain chocolate, broken into pieces

4 tbsp double cream

15 g/½ oz unsalted butter

pinch of salt

1. Preheat the oven to 180°C/350°F/Gas Mark 4 and line a 12-hole cupcake tin with paper cases.

2. Sift together the flour, cocoa powder, baking powder and salt in a bowl. Put the butter and caster sugar into a separate bowl and beat until pale and fluffy. Add the vanilla extract, then add the eggs, one at a time, beating after each addition. Add half of the flour mixture and the cream, and beat until incorporated. Add the remaining flour mixture and mix. Stir in the chocolate chips.

3. Spoon the batter into the paper cases and bake in the preheated oven for 20 minutes, until risen and a cocktail stick inserted into the centre of a cupcake comes out clean. Leave to cool in the tin for 1–2 minutes, then transfer to a wire rack to cool completely.

4. To make the frosting, put the butter into a bowl and beat with an electric mixer until it is pale and creamy. Add the icing sugar, milk, liqueur and vanilla extract. Beat together until well combined. Add more icing sugar, if necessary, to achieve a piping consistency. Spoon the frosting into a piping bag fitted with a star-shaped tip and pipe onto the cupcakes.

5. To make the chocolate sauce, place the chocolate, cream, butter and salt in a heatproof bowl set over a saucepan of gently simmering water and stir until the chocolate has completely melted. Set aside to cool for at least 15 minutes. To serve, lightly drizzle the chocolate sauce over the frosted cupcakes and sprinkle with chocolate chips.

Top tip

For a super-sweet tooth, swap the plain chocolate chips for white chocolate chips, and try hazelnut-flavoured Irish cream in the frosting.

Chocolate & Stout Cupcakes

makes 12

125 g/4½ oz plain flour

60 g/2¼ oz cocoa powder

1½ tsp baking powder

¼ tsp salt

115 g/4 oz unsalted butter, softened

200 g/7 oz caster sugar

1 tsp vanilla extract

2 large eggs

125 ml/4 fl oz stout

frosting

3 large egg whites

160 g/5¾ oz soft light brown sugar

160 g/5¾ oz unsalted butter, softened

1½ tsp vanilla extract

to decorate

55 g/2 oz green ready-to-roll fondant icing

icing sugar, for dusting

green sugar crystals

1. Preheat the oven to 180°C/350°F/Gas Mark 4 and line a 12-hole cupcake tin with paper cases.

2. Sift together the flour, cocoa powder, baking powder and salt in a bowl. Put the butter and caster sugar into a separate bowl and beat with an electric mixer until pale and fluffy. Add the vanilla extract, then add the eggs, one at a time, beating after each addition. Add half of the flour mixture and the stout, and beat until incorporated. Add the remaining flour mixture and mix.

3. Spoon the batter into the paper cases and bake in the preheated oven for 20 minutes, until risen and a cocktail stick inserted into the centre of a cupcake comes out clean. Leave to cool in the tin for 1–2 minutes, then transfer to a wire rack to cool completely.

4. To make the frosting, put the egg whites and brown sugar in a heatproof bowl set over a saucepan of gently simmering water and whisk until the sugar has completely dissolved. Remove from the heat and whisk the mixture for 4–5 minutes. Add the butter, 2 tablespoons at a time, and continue to whisk until it holds stiff peaks. Add the vanilla extract and beat until just combined. Spoon the frosting into a piping bag fitted with a star-shaped tip and pipe onto the cupcakes.

5. To make the clover decorations, roll out the fondant icing on a work surface lightly dusted with icing sugar until it is 5 mm/¼ inch thick. Cut out 12 clover shapes and set aside to dry.

6. Place a clover leaf on top of each cupcake and sprinkle with green sugar crystals.

Top tip

Swap the stout in the batter for alcohol-free root beer. This will give a sweeter, slightly spice-flavoured cake.

Limoncello Cupcakes

makes 12

190 g/6¾ oz plain flour

1½ tsp baking powder

¼ tsp salt

115 g/4 oz unsalted butter,
softened

200 g/7 oz caster sugar

2 large eggs

finely grated rind and juice of
1 lemon

4 tbsp milk

hundreds and thousands,
to decorate

frosting

3 large egg whites

150 g/5½ oz granulated sugar

225 g/8 oz unsalted butter,
softened

4 tbsp limoncello

finely grated rind of 1 lemon

1. Preheat the oven to 180°C/350°F/Gas Mark 4 and line a 12-hole cupcake tin with paper cases.

2. Sift together the flour, baking powder and salt in a bowl. Put the butter and caster sugar into a separate bowl and beat until pale and fluffy. Add the eggs, one at a time, beating after each addition. Add half of the flour mixture, the lemon rind and juice and the milk and beat until incorporated. Add the remaining flour mixture and mix.

3. Spoon the batter into the paper cases and bake in the preheated oven for 20 minutes, until risen and golden. Remove from the oven and leave to cool in the tin for 1–2 minutes, then transfer to a wire rack to cool completely.

4. To make the frosting, put the egg whites and granulated sugar in a heatproof bowl set over a saucepan of gently simmering water and whisk until the sugar has completely dissolved. Remove from the heat and whisk the mixture for 4–5 minutes. Add the butter, 2 tablespoons at a time, and continue to beat until it holds stiff peaks. Add the limoncello and lemon rind and beat until just combined.

5. Spoon the frosting into a piping bag fitted with a star-shaped tip and pipe onto the cupcakes. Sprinkle with hundreds and thousands.

3

4

5

Raspberry Daiquiri Cupcakes

makes 12

190 g/6¾ oz plain flour

1½ tsp baking powder

¼ tsp salt

115 g/4 oz unsalted butter, softened

200 g/7 oz caster sugar

2 large eggs

125 ml/4 fl oz milk

2 tbsp rum

finely grated rind and juice of 1 lime

pink sugar crystals, to decorate

filling

350 g/12 oz fresh raspberries, puréed

55 g/2 oz caster sugar

2 tbsp rum

1 tbsp cornflour

frosting

115 g/4 oz unsalted butter, softened

about 250 g/9 oz icing sugar (see method)

1 tsp raspberry extract

2 tbsp double cream

pinch of salt

1. Preheat the oven to 180°C/350°F/Gas Mark 4 and line a 12-hole cupcake tin with paper cases.

2. Sift together the flour, baking powder and salt in a bowl. Put the butter and caster sugar into a separate bowl and beat until pale and fluffy. Add the eggs, one at a time, beating after each addition. Add half of the flour mixture, the milk, rum and lime rind and juice and beat until incorporated. Add the remaining flour mixture and mix.

3. Spoon the batter into the paper cases and bake in the preheated oven for 20 minutes, until risen and golden. Leave to cool in the tin for 1–2 minutes, then transfer to a wire rack to cool completely.

4. To make the filling, put the raspberry purée and caster sugar in a saucepan and bring to the boil, stirring frequently. Put the rum and cornflour into a small bowl and whisk together. Pour into the boiling raspberry mixture and cook for a further 1–2 minutes, stirring, until the mixture thickens. Remove from the heat and cool, then chill.

5. To make the frosting, use an electric mixer to beat the butter until it is pale and creamy. Add the remaining ingredients and 2 tablespoons of the raspberry filling. Beat together until well combined. Add more icing sugar, if necessary, to achieve a piping consistency. Spoon the frosting into a piping bag fitted with a star-shaped tip.

6. Use an apple corer to remove the centre of each cupcake and spoon the raspberry filling into each hole. Pipe the frosting onto the cupcakes and then sprinkle with the sugar crystals.

Caramel Appletini Cupcakes

makes 12

190 g/6¾ oz plain flour

1½ tsp baking powder

1 tsp ground ginger

1 tsp ground cinnamon

⅛ tsp ground nutmeg

¼ tsp salt

115 g/4 oz unsalted butter, softened

200 g/7 oz caster sugar

1 tsp vanilla extract

2 large eggs

4 tbsp apple sauce

2 tbsp apple juice

2 tbsp apple-flavoured vodka

frosting

115 g/4 oz unsalted butter

200 g/7 oz soft dark brown sugar

90 ml/3 fl oz double cream

pinch of salt

2 tbsp apple-flavoured vodka

about 190 g/6¾ oz icing sugar (see method)

to decorate

green food colouring

55 g/2 oz marzipan

30 g/1 oz brown ready-to-roll fondant icing

1. Preheat the oven to 180°C/350°F/Gas Mark 4 and line a 12-hole cupcake tin with paper cases.

2. Sift together the flour, baking powder, ginger, cinnamon, nutmeg and salt in a bowl. Put the butter and caster sugar into a separate bowl and beat until pale and fluffy. Add the vanilla extract, then add the eggs, one at a time, beating after each addition. Add half of the flour mixture and the apple sauce, apple juice and vodka and beat to incorporate. Add the remaining flour mixture and mix.

3. Spoon the batter into the paper cases and bake in the preheated oven for 20 minutes, until risen and golden. Leave to cool in the tin for 1–2 minutes, then transfer to a wire rack to cool completely.

4. To make the frosting, first prepare a caramel sauce by melting the butter in a small saucepan over a medium heat. Add the brown sugar, cream and salt and cook, stirring constantly, for about 4 minutes, until the sugar has completely dissolved. Remove from the heat, stir in the vodka and set aside to cool for 30 minutes.

5. Pour the caramel sauce into a mixing bowl, reserving 125 ml/4 fl oz to decorate the cupcakes. Add the icing sugar to the mixing bowl and beat until fully incorporated. Add more icing sugar, if necessary, to achieve a piping consistency. Spoon the frosting into a piping bag fitted with a star-shaped tip and pipe onto the cupcakes.

6. To make the marzipan apple decorations, add a couple of drops of food colouring to the marzipan and knead until the colour is evenly incorporated. Roll the marzipan into 12 balls. Pinch off a small amount of fondant icing and shape into an apple stem. Press into the top of a marzipan ball and repeat for the 11 remaining balls. To serve, drizzle the cupcakes with the reserved caramel sauce and place a marzipan apple on top of each.

4

Top tip

Serve the cupcakes as a dessert — hot from the oven with the freshly made caramel sauce and a scoop of vanilla ice cream instead of the frosting.

6

6

White Russian Cupcakes

makes 12

190 g/6¾ oz plain flour

1½ tsp baking powder

¼ tsp salt

115 g/4 oz unsalted butter, softened

200 g/7 oz caster sugar

2 tsp vanilla extract

2 large eggs

90 ml/3 fl oz milk

4 tbsp coffee liqueur

frosting

115 g/4 oz unsalted butter, softened

about 375 g/13 oz icing sugar (see method)

1 tsp vanilla extract

2 tbsp vanilla-flavoured vodka

2 tbsp coffee liqueur

2 tbsp cocoa powder

1. Preheat the oven to 180°C/350°F/Gas Mark 4 and line a 12-hole cupcake tin with paper cases.

2. Sift together the flour, baking powder and salt in a bowl. Put the butter and caster sugar into a separate bowl and beat until pale and fluffy. Add the vanilla extract, then add the eggs, one at a time, beating after each addition. Add half of the flour mixture, the milk and liqueur and beat until incorporated. Add the remaining flour mixture and mix.

3. Spoon the batter into the paper cases and bake in the preheated oven for 20 minutes, until risen and golden. Leave to cool in the tin for 1–2 minutes, then transfer to a wire rack to cool completely.

4. To make the frosting, put the butter, icing sugar and vanilla extract into a bowl and beat with an electric mixer until well combined. Transfer half of the frosting to a separate bowl.

5. Add the vodka to one of the bowls of frosting and beat until well combined. Add more icing sugar, if necessary, to achieve a piping consistency. Spoon the frosting into a piping bag and set aside.

6. Add the coffee liqueur and cocoa powder to the other bowl of frosting and beat until well combined. Add more icing sugar, if necessary, to achieve a piping consistency. Spoon the frosting into a separate piping bag.

7. Put both piping bags side by side into a larger piping bag fitted with a star-shaped tip. Pipe the frosting onto the cupcakes.

Top tip

Push the frosting to the very tip
of the bags before piping onto
the cupcakes, to get a smooth
frosted finish.

4

7

7

Malibu Bay Cupcakes

makes 12

125 ml/4 fl oz cranberry juice

2 tbsp granulated sugar

190 g/6¾ oz plain flour

1½ tsp baking powder

¼ tsp salt

115 g/4 oz unsalted butter, softened

200 g/7 oz caster sugar

2 large eggs

125 ml/4 fl oz unsweetened coconut cream

2 tbsp white rum

20 g/¾ oz dried cranberries, chopped

frosting

3 large egg whites

150 g/5½ oz granulated sugar

225 g/8 oz unsalted butter, softened

3 tbsp white rum

1 tbsp coconut extract

to decorate

40 g/1½ oz sweetened desiccated coconut

pink food colouring

12 cocktail straws

1. Preheat the oven to 180°C/350°F/Gas Mark 4 and line a 12-hole cupcake tin with paper cases.

2. Combine the cranberry juice and granulated sugar in a small saucepan and bring to the boil over a medium–high heat. Boil for about 10 minutes, until reduced to about 2 tablespoons. Set aside to cool.

3. Sift together the flour, baking powder and salt in a bowl. Put the butter and caster sugar into a separate bowl and beat until pale and fluffy. Add the eggs, one at a time, beating after each addition. Add half of the flour mixture, the cooled cranberry reduction, coconut cream and rum, and beat until incorporated. Add the remaining flour mixture and mix. Stir in the dried cranberries.

4. Spoon the batter into the paper cases and bake in the preheated oven for 20 minutes, until risen and golden. Leave to cool in the tin for 1–2 minutes, then transfer to a wire rack to cool completely.

5. To make the frosting, put the egg whites and granulated sugar in a heatproof bowl set over a saucepan of gently simmering water and whisk until the sugar has completely dissolved. Remove from the heat and whisk the mixture for 4–5 minutes. Add the butter, 2 tablespoons at a time, and continue to beat until it holds stiff peaks. Add the rum and coconut extract and beat until just combined. Spoon the frosting into a piping bag fitted with a star-shaped tip and pipe onto the cupcakes.

6. To decorate, combine the coconut with a few drops of the food colouring and mix until the colour is evenly distributed. Sprinkle over the frosted cupcakes, and insert a cocktail straw into each.

Top tip

To evenly colour the desiccated
coconut, place in a polythene bag with
a few drops of the food colouring and
shake vigorously to combine.

Strawberry Mimosa Cupcakes

makes 12

190 g/6¾ oz plain flour

1½ tsp baking powder

¼ tsp salt

115 g/4 oz unsalted butter, softened

200 g/7 oz caster sugar

1 tsp vanilla extract

2 large eggs

125 ml/4 fl oz champagne or other sparkling wine

finely grated rind of 1 orange

2 tbsp orange juice

filling

4 tbsp water

2 tbsp cornflour

175 g/6 oz frsh strawberries, diced

75 g/2¾ oz icing sugar

4 tbsp champagne or other sparkling wine

frosting

115 g/4 oz unsalted butter, softened

about 440 g/15¾ oz icing sugar (see method)

4 tbsp champagne, or other sparkling wine

finely grated rind of 1 orange

2 tbsp orange juice

1. Preheat the oven to 180°C/350°F/Gas Mark 4 and line a 12-hole cupcake tin with paper cases.

2. Sift together the flour, baking powder and salt in a bowl. Put the butter and caster sugar into a separate bowl and beat until pale and fluffy. Add the vanilla extract, then add the eggs, one at a time, beating after each addition. Add half of the flour mixture and the champagne and beat until combined. Add the remaining flour mixture, the orange rind and orange juice and mix.

3. Spoon the batter into the paper cases and bake in the preheated oven for 20 minutes, until risen and golden. Leave to cool in the tin for 1–2 minutes, then transfer to a wire rack to cool completely.

4. To make the filling, stir the water and cornflour together in a saucepan and bring to the boil over a medium–high heat, stirring. Add the strawberries and icing sugar, reduce the heat to low and simmer, stirring frequently, for 5 minutes, until the mixture has thickened. Add the champagne and continue to simmer for a further 3–5 minutes, until the mixture has thickened. Set aside to cool.

5. To make the frosting, put the butter, icing sugar, champagne, orange rind, orange juice and salt into a bowl and beat with an electric mixer until well combined. Add more icing sugar, if necessary, to achieve a piping consistency. Spoon into a piping bag fitted with a star-shaped tip.

to decorate

115 g/4 oz marzipan
red food colouring
yellow food colouring
orange edible-ink marker
pink sugar crystals

6. To make the orange wedge decorations, divide the marzipan in half. Add a few drops of red food colouring and a few drops of yellow food colouring to one half of the marzipan and knead until evenly incorporated. Add more colour if needed to achieve a dark orange colour – this will be used to make the orange rind. Add a couple of drops of yellow food colouring and a couple of drops of red food colouring to the remaining piece of marzipan and knead until evenly incorporated – this will be used to make the inside of the orange wedges.

7. Divide both marzipan colours into 12 pieces. Take one piece of light orange marzipan and shape into a semi-circle about 5 mm/¼ inch thick. Lightly pinch the flat side of the semi-circle to make a wedge shape. Flatten a piece of the dark orange marzipan and press in place around the curved edge of the wedge, trimming as necessary to give the effect of a rind. Repeat with the remaining marzipan to make 12 orange wedges in total. Using the edible-ink marker, draw lines on the lighter orange part to represent the inner membrane of an orange wedge. Set aside to dry.

8. Use an apple corer to remove the centre of each cupcake. Spoon the strawberry filling into the holes. Pipe the frosting onto the cupcakes, sprinkle with sugar crystals, then top each cupcake with a marzipan orange wedge.

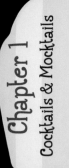

4

Top tip

For a non-alcoholic version, substitute carbonated orange drink for the champagne in the cupcake batter, filling and frosting and omit the orange rind and juice.

8

8

Cola Cupcakes

makes 12

190 g/6¾ oz plain flour

1½ tsp baking powder

¼ tsp salt

115 g/4 oz unsalted butter, softened

150 g/5½ oz caster sugar

100 g/3½ oz soft dark brown sugar

1 tsp vanilla extract

2 large eggs

125 ml/4 fl oz cola syrup

4 tbsp soured cream

frosting

115 g/4 oz unsalted butter

200 g/7 oz soft dark brown sugar

6 tbsp double cream

½ tsp salt

about 190 g/6¾ oz icing sugar (see method)

1. Preheat the oven to 180°C/350°F/Gas Mark 4 and line a 12-hole cupcake tin with paper cases.

2. Sift together the flour, baking powder and salt in a bowl. Put the butter, caster sugar and brown sugar into a separate bowl and beat until pale and fluffy. Add the vanilla extract, then add the eggs, one at a time, beating after each addition. Add half of the flour mixture, the cola syrup and soured cream and beat until well combined. Add the remaining flour mixture and mix.

3. Spoon the batter into the paper cases and bake in the preheated oven for 20 minutes, until risen and a cocktail stick inserted into the centre of a cupcake comes out clean. Leave to cool in the tin for 1–2 minutes, then transfer to a wire rack to cool completely.

4. To make the frosting, first prepare a caramel sauce by putting the butter into a small saucepan and melting over a medium heat. Add the brown sugar, cream and salt and cook, stirring constantly, for 4 minutes, or until the sugar has completely dissolved. Remove from the heat and set aside to cool for 30 minutes.

5. Transfer the caramel sauce to a bowl and beat in the icing sugar. Add more icing sugar, if necessary, to achieve a piping consistency. Transfer to a piping bag fitted with a star-shaped tip and pipe onto the cupcakes.

Top tip

For a true American soda-shop
finish, top the cupcakes with a glacé
cherry and red and white striped paper
straws, cut to length.

Vanilla Chai Tea Cupcakes

makes 12

125 ml/4 fl oz milk

3 chai tea bags

190 g/6¾ oz plain flour

1½ tsp baking powder

¼ tsp each ground cinnamon, ground ginger, ground nutmeg and ground allspice, mixed

¼ tsp salt

115 g/4 oz unsalted butter, softened

200 g/7 oz caster sugar

1 tsp vanilla extract

2 large eggs

1 tsp ground cinnamon and 1 tbsp granulated sugar, mixed, to decorate

frosting

3 large egg whites

150 g/5½ oz granulated sugar

225 g/8 oz unsalted butter, softened

1 tsp vanilla extract

1 tsp ground cinnamon

pinch of salt

1. Preheat the oven to 180°C/350°F/Gas Mark 4 and line a 12-hole cupcake tin with paper cases.

2. Heat the milk in a small saucepan until just boiling. Add the tea bags, remove from the heat and leave to steep for 15 minutes. Remove and discard the tea bags and set the milk aside to cool completely.

3. Sift together the flour, baking powder, mixed spices and salt in a bowl. Put the butter and caster sugar into a separate bowl and beat until pale and fluffy. Add the vanilla extract, then add the eggs, one at a time, beating after each addition, until combined. Add half of the flour mixture and the tea-infused milk and beat until combined. Add the remaining flour and mix.

4. Spoon the batter into the prepared paper cases and bake in the preheated oven for 20 minutes, until risen and golden. Leave to cool in the tin for 1–2 minutes, then transfer to a wire rack to cool completely.

5. To make the frosting, put the egg whites and granulated sugar in a heatproof bowl set over a saucepan of gently simmering water and whisk until the sugar has completely dissolved. Remove from the heat and whisk the mixture for 4–5 minutes. Add the butter, 2 tablespoons at a time, and continue to beat until it holds stiff peaks. Add the vanilla extract and cinnamon and beat until just combined. Spoon the frosting into a piping bag fitted with a star-shaped tip and pipe onto the cupcakes.

6. To decorate, sprinkle the cinnamon-sugar over the top of the cupcakes.

2

5

6

Pink Lemonade Cupcakes

makes 10

115 g/4 oz self-raising flour

¼ tsp baking powder

115 g/4 oz unsalted butter, softened

115 g/4 oz caster sugar

2 eggs

pink food colouring

55 g/2 oz granulated sugar

juice of 1 lemon

pink, white and red sugar sprinkles and 10 pink drinking straws, to decorate

frosting

115 g/4 oz unsalted butter, softened

finely grated rind and juice of ½ lemon

4 tbsp double cream

225 g/8 oz icing sugar

pink food colouring

1. Preheat the oven to 180°C/350°F/Gas Mark 4. and line a 10-hole cupcake tin with paper cases.

2. Sift together the flour and baking powder in a bowl. Put the butter and caster sugar into a separate bowl and beat until pale and fluffy. Add the eggs, one at a time, beating after each addition. Add half of the flour mixture and several drops of food colouring and mix until combined. Add the remaining flour mixture and mix.

3. Spoon the batter into the paper cases and bake in the preheated oven for 20 minutes, until risen and golden. Leave to cool slightly in the tin.

4. Meanwhile, place the granulated sugar and lemon juice in a saucepan over a medium heat and heat, stirring, until the sugar has dissolved. Prick the tops of the warm cupcakes all over with a skewer and brush the cupcakes with the lemon syrup. Transfer to a wire rack to cool completely.

5. To make the frosting, put the butter, lemon rind and juice, cream and icing sugar in a bowl and beat with an electric mixer until well combined. Add a few drops of food colouring and mix until evenly incorporated.

6. Use a palette knife to spread frosting over the tops of the cupcakes. Spread the sugar sprinkles out on a flat plate and edge the frosting with sugar sprinkles, then insert a drinking straw into each.

Top tip

For a fun finishing touch, try edging the frosting-topped cupcakes in strawberry-flavoured popping candy.

6

6

6

51

CHAPTER 2
FEISTY
FLAVOURS

Maple & Bacon Cupcakes

makes 12

190 g/6¾ oz plain flour

1½ tsp baking powder

¼ tsp salt

115 g/4 oz unsalted butter,
softened

100 g/3½ oz caster sugar

125 ml/4 fl oz maple syrup

1 tsp vanilla extract

2 large eggs

125 ml/4 fl oz milk

candied bacon

8 rashers unsmoked streaky
bacon

55 g/2 oz soft light brown sugar

frosting

4 large egg whites

200 g/7 oz granulated sugar

¼ tsp cream of tartar

2 tbsp maple syrup

2 tsp maple extract

1. Preheat the oven to 180°C/350°F/Gas Mark 4 and line a 12-hole cupcake tin with paper cases.

2. To make the candied bacon, line a baking sheet with foil. Place the bacon on the prepared sheet and sprinkle half of the sugar over. Turn and repeat. Bake in the preheated oven for 25–30 minutes, until the bacon is crisp (do not switch off the oven). Transfer to kitchen paper and leave to cool. Reserve 4 whole rashers of bacon for decoration and crumble the remaining bacon.

3. Sift together the flour, baking powder and salt in a bowl. Put the butter and caster sugar into a separate bowl and beat until pale and fluffy. Add the maple syrup and vanilla extract, then add the eggs, one at a time, beating after each addition. Add half of the flour mixture and the milk and beat until combined. Add the remaining flour mixture and mix. Stir in the crumbled candied bacon.

4. Spoon the batter into the paper cases and bake in the oven for 20 minutes, until risen and golden. Leave to cool in the tin for 1–2 minutes, then transfer to a wire rack to cool completely.

5. To make the frosting, put the egg whites, granulated sugar and cream of tartar in a heatproof bowl set over a saucepan of gently simmering water and whisk until the sugar is completely dissolved. Remove from the heat and whisk the mixture for 4–5 minutes or until it holds stiff peaks. Add the maple syrup and maple extract and whisk until combined. Spoon the frosting into a piping bag fitted with a star-shaped tip and pipe onto the cupcakes. Break the reserved candied bacon into 12 pieces and place on top of the cupcakes.

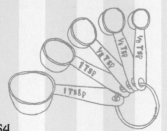

Top tip

Spice up your cupcakes —
sprinkle 1½ teaspoons of
ground cinnamon over the
bacon rashers before baking.

4

5

5

Chocolate Chip Cookie Cupcakes

makes 12

250 g/9 oz uncooked ready-made chocolate chip cookie dough

190 g/6¾ oz plain flour

1½ tsp baking powder

¼ tsp salt

115 g/4 oz unsalted butter, softened

50 g/1¾ oz caster sugar

100 g/3½ oz soft light brown sugar

2 tsp vanilla extract

2 large eggs

125 ml/4 fl oz milk

50 g/1¾ oz plain chocolate chips, to decorate

frosting

3 large egg whites

160 g/5¾ oz sofr light brown sugar

160 g/5¾ oz unsalted butter, softened

1½ tsp vanilla extract

1. Preheat the oven to 190°C/375°F/Gas Mark 5 and line a 12-hole cupcake tin with paper cases.

2. Drop rounded spoonfuls of cookie dough into the paper cases and bake in the preheated oven for 8–10 minutes, or until the cookies have begun to brown. Remove from the oven and reduce the oven temperature to 180°C/350°F/Gas Mark 4.

3. Sift together the flour, baking powder and salt in a bowl. Put the butter, caster sugar and brown sugar into a separate bowl and beat until pale and fluffy. Add the vanilla extract, then add the eggs, one at a time, beating after each addition. Add half of the flour mixture and the milk and beat until incorporated. Add the remaining flour mixture and mix.

4. Spoon the batter on top of the cookie bases and bake for 20 minutes, until risen and a cocktail stick inserted into the centre of a cupcake comes out clean. Leave to cool in the tin for 1–2 minutes, then transfer to a wire rack to cool completely.

5. To make the frosting, put the egg whites and brown sugar in a heatproof bowl set over a saucepan of gently simmering water and whisk until the sugar is completely dissolved. Remove from the heat and whisk the mixture for 4–5 minutes. Add the butter, 2 tablespoons at a time, and continue to beat until it holds stiff peaks. Add the vanilla extract and beat until just combined. Spoon the frosting into a piping bag fitted with a star-shaped tip and pipe onto the cupcakes, then sprinkle with chocolate chips.

Top tip

Instead of cookie dough, you could
place a small ready-baked biscuit or
cookie in the bottom of the paper cases
and skip the first baking step.

Pink Lemon Meringue Cupcakes

makes 12

200 g/7 oz plain flour

1½ tsp baking powder

¼ tsp salt

115 g/4 oz unsalted butter, softened

200 g/7 oz caster sugar

1 tsp vanilla extract

2 large eggs

finely grated rind and juice of 1 lemon

4 tbsp milk

pink food colouring

filling

225 ml/8 oz lemon curd

125 ml/4 fl oz double cream, whipped

frosting

4 large egg whites

200 g/7 oz granulated sugar

¼ tsp cream of tartar

1 tbsp lemon juice

1 tsp lemon extract

pink food colouring

1. Preheat the oven to 180°C/350°F/Gas Mark 4 and line a 12-hole cupcake tin with paper cases.

2. Sift together the flour, baking powder and salt in a bowl. Put the butter and caster sugar into a separate bowl and beat until pale and fluffy. Add the vanilla extract, then add the eggs, one at a time, beating after each addition. Add half of the flour mixture, the lemon rind and juice and the milk, and beat until combined. Add the remaining flour mixture and mix. Add a few drops of food colouring and stir until evenly incorporated.

3. Spoon the batter into the paper cases and bake in the preheated oven for 20 minutes, until risen and golden. Leave to cool in the tin for 1–2 minutes, then transfer to a wire rack to cool completely.

4. To make the filling, gently fold the lemon curd into the whipped cream and chill until ready to use.

5. Use an apple corer to remove the centre of each cupcake. Spoon the lemon curd filling into the holes.

6. To make the frosting, put the egg whites, granulated sugar and cream of tartar in a heatproof bowl set over a saucepan of gently simmering water and whisk until the sugar has completely dissolved. Remove from the heat and whisk the mixture for 4–5 minutes, until it holds stiff peaks. Add the lemon juice, lemon extract and a few drops of food colouring and beat until combined.

7. Spoon the frosting into a piping bag fitted with a large round tip and pipe onto the cupcakes.

Fluffy Gingerbread Cupcakes

makes 12

190 g/6¾ oz plain flour

1½ tsp baking powder

2 tsp ground ginger

1 tsp ground cinnamon

¼ tsp ground allspice

¼ tsp ground nutmeg

¼ tsp salt

115 g/4 oz unsalted butter, softened

110 g/3¾ oz soft dark brown sugar

1 tsp vanilla extract

2 large eggs

160 g/5¾ oz treacle

125 ml/4 fl oz milk

55 g/2 oz brown ready-to-roll fondant icing and black edible-ink marker, to decorate

icing sugar, for dusting

Frosting

175 g/6 oz cream cheese

55 g/2 oz butter, softened

about 500 g/1 lb 2 oz icing sugar (see method)

1 tsp ground ginger

finely grated rind of 1 lemon

2 tbsp lemon juice

pinch of salt

1. Preheat the oven to 180°C/350°F/Gas Mark 4 and line a 12-hole cupcake tin with paper cases.

2. Sift together the flour, baking powder, ginger, cinnamon, allspice, nutmeg and salt in a bowl. Put the butter and brown sugar into a separate bowl and beat until pale and fluffy. Add the vanilla extract, then add the eggs, one at a time, beating after each addition. Add half of the flour mixture and the treacle and milk and mix to incorporate. Add the remaining flour mixture and mix.

3. Spoon the batter into the paper cases and bake in the preheated oven for 20 minutes, until risen and a cocktail stick inserted into the centre of a cupcake comes out clean. Leave to cool in the tin for 1–2 minutes, then transfer to a wire rack to cool completely.

4. To make the frosting, combine the cream cheese, butter, icing sugar, ginger, lemon rind, lemon juice and salt in a bowl and mix with an electric mixer until well combined. Add more icing sugar, if necessary, to achieve a piping consistency. Spoon the frosting into a piping bag fitted with a medium star-shaped tip and pipe onto the cupcakes.

5. To decorate, roll out the fondant icing on a work surface lightly dusted with icing sugar until it is 5 mm/¼ inch thick. Cut out 12 mini gingerbread men shapes and set aside on a sheet of baking paper to dry. Once hardened, use the edible-ink marker to draw on eyes, mouths and buttons. To serve, place a gingerbread man on top of each cupcake.

Chocolate & Pink Pepper Cupcakes

makes 12

125 g/4½ oz plain flour

60 g/2¼ oz cocoa powder

1 tsp baking powder

¼ tsp salt

115 g/4 oz unsalted butter, softened

200 g/7 oz caster sugar

2 tsp vanilla extract

2 large eggs

125 ml/4 fl oz soured cream

1 tbsp pink peppercorns, crushed, to decorate

Frosting

4 tbsp milk

1 tbsp pink peppercorns, crushed

115 g/4 oz unsalted butter, softened

about 250 g/9 oz icing sugar (see method)

2 tsp vanilla extract

1. Preheat the oven to 180°C/350°F/Gas Mark 4 and line a 12-hole cupcake tin with paper cases.

2. Sift together the flour, cocoa powder, baking powder and salt in a bowl. Put the butter and caster sugar into a separate bowl and beat until pale and fluffy. Add the vanilla extract, then add the eggs, one at a time, beating after each addition. Add half of the flour mixture and the soured cream and beat until combined. Add the remaining flour mixture and mix.

3. Spoon the batter into the paper cases and bake in the preheated oven for 20 minutes, until risen and a cocktail stick inserted into the centre of a cupcake comes out clean. Leave to cool in the tin for 1–2 minutes, then transfer to a wire rack to cool completely.

4. To make the frosting, put the milk and peppercorns into a small saucepan and heat over a medium heat until just boiling. Reduce the heat to low and simmer for about 5 minutes, stirring frequently. Strain the milk into a bowl, discarding the peppercorns, and leave to cool for about 10 minutes.

5. Add the butter, icing sugar and vanilla extract to the milk and beat using an electric mixer until well combined. Add more icing sugar, if necessary, to achieve a piping consistency. Spoon the frosting into a piping bag fitted with a star-shaped tip and pipe onto the cupcakes.

6. To decorate, sprinkle a little pink pepper over the top of the cupcakes.

Top tip

If you don't have a pestle and
mortar, place the peppercorns
in a polythene bag and crush
them with a rolling pin.

4

5

6

Pomegranate & Green Tea Cupcakes

makes 12

190 g/6¾ oz plain flour

1½ tsp baking powder

1 tbsp green tea powder

½ tsp salt

115 g/4 oz unsalted butter, softened

200 g/7 oz caster sugar

1 tsp vanilla extract

2 large eggs

4 tbsp milk

pomegranate seeds, to decorate

pomegranate syrup

475 ml/17 fl oz pomegranate juice

100 g/3½ oz caster sugar

frosting

115 g/4 oz unsalted butter, softened

about 300 g/10½ oz icing sugar (see method)

1. To make the pomegranate syrup, put the pomegranate juice and the sugar into a saucepan and bring to the boil over a medium-high heat, stirring occasionally, until the sugar has dissolved. Reduce the heat to low and cook until the mixture has reduced to about 125 ml/4 fl oz. Set aside to cool.

2. Preheat the oven to 180°C/350°F/Gas Mark 4. Line a 12-hole cupcake tin with paper cases.

3. Sift together the flour, baking powder, green tea powder and salt in a bowl. Put the butter and caster sugar into a separate bowl and beat until pale and fluffy. Add the vanilla extract, then add the eggs, one at a time, beating after each addition. Add half of the flour mixture, 4 tablespoons of the pomegranate syrup and the milk and mix to incorporate. Add the remaining flour mixture and mix.

4. Spoon the batter into the paper cases and bake in the preheated oven for 20 minutes, or until a cocktail stick inserted into the centre of a cupcake comes out clean. Leave to cool in the tin for 1–2 minutes, then transfer to a wire rack to cool completely.

5. To make the frosting, put the butter, icing sugar and remaining pomegranate syrup in a bowl and beat with an electric mixer until well combined. Add more icing sugar, if necessary, to achieve a piping consistency. Spoon the frosting into a piping bag fitted with a star-shaped tip and pipe onto the cupcakes.

6. To decorate, sprinkle the pomegranate seeds over the cupcakes.

Coffee & Doughnuts Cupcakes

makes 12

250 g/9 oz plain flour

60 g/2¼ oz cocoa powder

2 tsp baking powder

¼ tsp salt

140 g/5 oz unsalted butter, softened, plus extra for greasing

300 g/10½ oz caster sugar

1 tbsp coffee extract

3 large eggs

125 ml/4 fl oz strong brewed coffee, cooled

125 ml/4 fl oz double cream

frosting

3 large egg whites

150 g/5½ oz granulated sugar

225 g/8 oz unsalted butter, softened

1 tbsp coffee extract

to decorate

225 g/8 oz chocolate coating, broken into pieces

2 tbsp vegetable oil

hundreds and thousands

1. Preheat the oven to 180°C/350°F/Gas Mark 4, line a 12-hole cupcake tin with paper cases and grease a 23-cm/9-inch round, shallow cake tin. Line a baking sheet with baking paper.

2. Sift together the flour, cocoa powder, baking powder and salt in a bowl. Put the butter and caster sugar into a separate bowl and beat until pale and fluffy. Add the coffee extract, then add the eggs, one at a time, beating between each addition. Add half of the flour mixture and the coffee and cream and beat until combined. Add the remaining flour mixture and mix.

3. Spoon the batter into the paper cases and transfer the remaining batter to the prepared cake tin, spreading out in an even layer. Bake in the preheated oven for 20 minutes, or until a cocktail stick inserted into the centre of a cupcake and the cake comes out clean (the cake may take a few minutes longer to cook through). Leave to cool in the tins for 1–2 minutes, then transfer to a wire rack to cool completely.

4. To make the frosting, put the egg whites and granulated sugar in a heatproof bowl set over a saucepan of gently simmering water and whisk until the sugar has completely dissolved. Remove from the heat and whisk the mixture for 4–5 minutes. Add the butter, 2 tablespoons at a time, and continue to whisk until it holds stiff peaks. Add the coffee extract and beat until combined. Spoon the frosting into a piping bag fitted with a star-shaped tip. Chill

until ready to use.

5. Use a 5-cm/2-inch round cutter to cut out 6 rounds from the cake. Chill in the freezer for about 30 minutes. Halve the rounds horizontally so that you have 12 rounds, each approximately 2 cm/¾ inch thick. Using an apple corer cut out and discard a hole from the centre of each round.

6. To make the chocolate coating, put the chocolate and oil in a heatproof bowl set over a saucepan of gently simmering water and stir until the chocolate has completely melted.

7. Dunk the cake rings into the chocolate coating by laying them, one at a time, on the tines of a fork and lowering them into the mixture. Let the excess run off, then place the coated doughnut on the prepared baking sheet and immediately sprinkle with hundreds and thousands. Repeat until all 12 doughnuts are coated and sprinkled. Place in the refrigerator and chill for about 15 minutes, until the chocolate has set.

8. To serve, remove the cases from the cupcakes and put a cupcake in each of 12 coffee cups. Pipe the frosting on top, then place a doughnut on top of each.

5

7

7

Top tip

Instead of coating the mini doughnuts in chocolate you could use candy melts, which are available in a range of bright colours.

Chilli Chocolate Cupcakes

makes 12

125 g/4½ oz plain flour

75 g/2¾ oz cocoa powder

1½ tsp baking powder

½ tsp ground cinnamon

1 tsp mild chilli powder

¼ tsp cayenne pepper

¼ tsp salt

115 g/4 oz unsalted butter,
softened

200 g/7 oz caster sugar

2 tsp vanilla extract

2 large eggs

125 ml/4 fl oz milk

2 squares plain chocolate, to
decorate

frosting

115 g/4 oz unsalted butter,
softened

about 190 g/6¾ oz icing sugar
(see method)

40 g/1½ oz cocoa powder

2 tbsp milk

1 tsp vanilla extract

1 tsp ground cinnamon

1. Preheat the oven to 180°C/350°F/Gas Mark 4 and line a 12-hole cupcake tin with paper cases.

2. Sift together the flour, cocoa powder, baking powder, cinnamon, chilli powder, cayenne pepper and salt in a bowl. Put the butter and caster sugar into a separate bowl and beat until pale and fluffy. Add the vanilla extract, then add the eggs, one at a time, beating after each addition. Add half of the flour mixture and the milk and beat until incorporated. Add the remaining flour mixture and mix.

3. Spoon the batter into the paper cases and bake in the preheated oven for 20 minutes, until risen and a cocktail stick inserted into the centre of a cupcake comes out clean. Leave to cool in the tin for 1–2 minutes, then transfer to a wire rack to cool completely.

4. To make the frosting, put the butter in a bowl and beat with an electric mixer until pale and fluffy. Add the icing sugar together with the cocoa powder, milk, vanilla extract and cinnamon. Beat together until well combined. Add more icing sugar, if necessary, to achieve a piping consistency. Spoon the frosting into a piping bag fitted with a star-shaped tip and pipe onto the cupcakes.

5. To decorate, grate the chocolate over the top of the cupcakes.

Baklava Cupcakes

makes 12

190 g/6¾ oz plain flour

1½ tsp baking powder

¾ tsp ground cinnamon

¼ tsp salt

115 g/4 oz unsalted butter, softened

125 ml/4 fl oz clear honey

100 g/3½ oz caster sugar

2 tsp vanilla extract

2 large eggs

125 ml/4 fl oz milk

30 g/1 oz chopped walnuts

30 g/1 oz chopped pistachio nuts

honey syrup

125 ml/4 fl oz clear honey

100 g/3½ oz caster sugar

4 tbsp water

1 strip of orange zest, about 1 x 7.5 cm/½ x 3 inches

filo rounds

60 g/2¼ oz unsalted butter, melted, plus extra for greasing

12 sheets filo pastry, thawed if frozen

1. To make the honey syrup, combine the ingredients in a small saucepan. Cook over a medium heat until the sugar has dissolved, then increase the heat to medium–high, bring to the boil and cook for about 6 minutes, or until the mixture becomes syrupy. Remove and discard the orange zest and set the syrup aside to cool.

2. To make the filo rounds, preheat the oven to 180°C/350°F/Gas Mark 4 and grease a baking sheet. Combine the melted butter with 4 tablespoons of the cooled honey syrup in a small bowl.

3. Lay 1 sheet of filo pastry flat on a large, clean work surface and brush with the butter-syrup mixture. Lay a second piece of pastry flat on top and brush it with the butter-syrup mixture. Continue until you have 6 layers of pastry, finishing with a coating of the butter-syrup mixture. Repeat with the remaining 6 sheets of pastry. Cut out 24 pastry rounds using a 5-cm/2-inch round cutter. Cut 12 of the rounds in half to make 24 semi-circles. Place the pastry shapes on the prepared baking sheet. Sprinkle lightly with cold water to prevent the pastry from curling.

4. Bake in the preheated oven for 7–10 minutes, or until the pastry circles are very light brown and crisp. Remove the circles from the oven, and bake the semi-circles for a further 1–2 minutes, until they are a light golden colour. Transfer to a wire rack to cool (do not switch off the oven).

frosting

115 g/4 oz unsalted butter, softened

90 ml/3 fl oz clear honey

250 g/9 oz icing sugar

honey-nut topping

30 g/1 oz finely chopped walnuts

30 g/1 oz finely chopped pistachio nuts

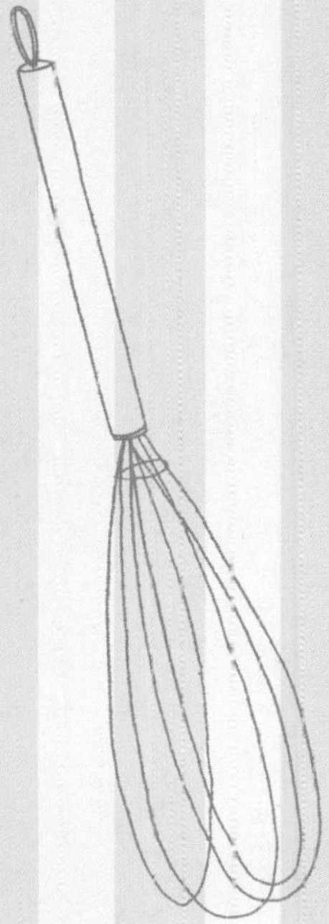

5. Line a 12-hole cupcake tin with paper cases and place one of the filo rounds in each case.

6. Sift together the flour, baking powder, cinnamon and salt in a bowl. Put the butter, honey and caster sugar into a separate bowl and beat until pale and fluffy. Add the vanilla extract, then add the eggs, one at a time, beating after each addition. Add half of the flour mixture and the milk and beat until combined. Add the remaining flour mixture and mix. Stir in the chopped nuts.

7. Spoon the batter into the paper cases on top of the filo rounds, and bake in the oven for about 20 minutes, until risen and golden. Leave to cool for 1-2 minutes, then transfer to a wire rack to cool completely.

8. To make the frosting, put the butter, honey and icing sugar into a bowl and beat until well combined. Use a palette knife to spread the frosting on top of the cupcakes.

9. To make the topping, put the chopped nuts into a small bowl with the remaining honey syrup and stir to combine. To serve, spoon the topping onto the cupcakes and place a couple of filo pastry semi-circles on top of each.

3

9

9

Top tip

Handle the delicate filo pastry gently, rolling it up and covering it with a damp tea towel while you work, to prevent it drying out.

Peanut Butter & Jelly Cupcakes

makes 12

190 g/6¾ oz plain flour

1½ tsp baking powder

¼ tsp salt

115 g/4 oz unsalted butter, softened

200 g/7 oz caster sugar

125 g/4½ oz smooth peanut butter

1 tsp vanilla extract

2 large eggs

125 ml/4 fl oz milk

325 g/11½ oz strawberry jam, at room temperature, plus extra to decorate

frosting

115 g/4 oz unsalted butter, softened

125 g/4½ oz smooth peanut butter

about 200 g/7 oz icing sugar (see method)

3 tbsp milk

pinch of salt

1. Preheat the oven to 180°C/350°F/Gas Mark 4 and line a 12-hole cupcake tin with paper cases.

2. Sift together the flour, baking powder and salt in a bowl. Put the butter and caster sugar into a separate bowl and beat until pale and fluffy. Add the peanut butter and beat until combined. Add the vanilla extract, then add the eggs, one at a time, beating after each addition. Add half of the flour mixture and the milk and beat until incorporated. Add the remaining flour mixture and mix.

3. Spoon the batter into the paper cases and bake in the preheated oven for 20 minutes, until risen and golden. Leave to cool in the tin for 1–2 minutes, then transfer to a wire rack to cool completely.

4. To make the frosting, put the butter and peanut butter into a bowl and beat with an electric mixer until pale and fluffy. Add the icing sugar, milk and salt and beat together until well combined. Add more icing sugar, if necessary, to achieve a piping consistency. Transfer to a piping bag fitted with a star-shaped tip.

5. Use an apple corer to remove the centre of each cupcake and spoon the jam into the holes. Pipe the frosting onto the cupcakes, leaving an indentation in the middle. Spoon a little of the jam into each indentation and serve.

Poached Pear Cupcakes

makes 12

1 litre/1¾ pints water

200 g/7 oz granulated sugar

3 small pears, peeled, quartered and cored

1 cinnamon stick

75 g/2¾ oz plain flour

70 g/2½ oz ground almonds

1 tsp baking powder

¼ tsp salt

115 g/4 oz unsalted butter, softened

200 g/7 oz caster sugar

2 tsp vanilla extract

2 large eggs

4 tbsp double cream

frosting

3 large egg whites

150 g/5½ oz icing sugar

225 g/8 oz unsalted butter, softened

1 tsp vanilla extract

1 tsp ground cinnamon

to decorate

115 g/4 oz marzipan

green and gold edible glitter

12 cloves

1. Bring the water and granulated sugar to the boil in a saucepan. Reduce the heat to low and simmer, stirring, until the sugar has dissolved. Add the pears and cinnamon stick and simmer for 20 minutes. Drain and set aside to cool. Preheat the oven to 180°C/350°F/Gas Mark 4 and line a 12-hole cupcake tin with paper cases.

2. Sift together the flour, ground almonds, baking powder and salt in a bowl. Put the butter and caster sugar into a separate bowl and beat until pale and fluffy. Add the vanilla extract, then add the eggs, one at a time, beating after each addition. Add half of the flour mixture and the cream and beat until incorporated. Add the remaining flour mixture and mix.

3. Spoon the batter into the paper cases and put a pear quarter into each. Bake in the preheated oven for 20 minutes, until risen and golden. Leave to cool in the tin for 1–2 minutes, then transfer to a wire rack to cool completely.

4. To make the frosting, put the egg whites and icing sugar in a heatproof bowl set over a saucepan of gently simmering water and whisk until the sugar has completely dissolved. Remove from the heat and whisk the mixture for 4–5 minutes. Add the butter, 2 tablespoons at a time, and continue to whisk until it holds stiff peaks. Add the vanilla extract and cinnamon and beat until just combined. Spoon the frosting into a piping bag fitted with a star-shaped tip and pipe onto the cupcakes.

5. To decorate, break the marzipan into 12 pieces and form each piece into a pear shape. Paint with the edible glitter and press a clove into the top of each to represent a stem. Top each cupcake with a marzipan pear.

Top tip

Reserve the poaching liquid from the pears and cook until reduced to a syrup — then drizzle over the cupcakes.

1

3

5

79

Salted Caramel Cupcakes

makes 12

190 g/6¾ oz plain flour

1½ tsp baking powder

¼ tsp salt

115 g/4 oz unsalted butter, softened

100 g/3½ oz caster sugar

110 g/3¾ oz soft dark brown sugar

1 tsp vanilla extract

1 tsp coffee extract

2 large eggs

125 ml/4 fl oz milk

1 tsp sea salt flakes, to decorate

frosting

115 g/4 oz unsalted butter

220 g/7¾ oz soft dark brown sugar

90 ml/3 fl oz double cream

½ tsp salt

about 190 g/6¾ oz icing sugar (see method)

1. Preheat the oven to 180°C/350°F/Gas Mark 4 and line a 12-hole cupcake tin with paper cases.

2. Sift together the flour, baking powder and salt in a bowl. Put the butter, caster sugar and brown sugar into a separate bowl and beat until pale and fluffy. Add the vanilla extract and coffee extract, then add the eggs one at a time, beating between each addition. Add half of the flour mixture and the milk and beat until incorporated. Add the remaining flour mixture and mix.

3. Spoon the batter into the paper cases and bake in the preheated oven for 20 minutes, until risen and golden. Leave to cool in the tin for 1–2 minutes, then transfer to a wire rack to cool completely.

4. To make the frosting, first prepare a caramel sauce by melting the butter in a small saucepan over a medium heat. Add the brown sugar, cream and salt and cook, stirring constantly, for about 4 minutes, or until the sugar is completely dissolved. Remove from the heat and set aside to cool.

5. Add the icing sugar to the caramel sauce and beat until fully incorporated. Add more icing sugar, if necessary, to achieve a piping consistency. Spoon into a piping bag fitted with a star-shaped tip and pipe onto the cupcakes.

6. To decorate, sprinkle the cupcakes with the salt flakes.

5

5

6

CHAPTER 3
FUN &
FROSTED

Watermelon Cupcakes

makes 12

190 g/6¾ oz plain flour

1½ tsp baking powder

¼ tsp salt

115 g/4 oz unsalted butter, softened

200 g/7 oz caster sugar

2 tsp vanilla extract

2 large eggs

125 ml/4 fl oz milk

pink food colouring

90 g/3¼ oz plain chocolate chips

frosting

115 g/4 oz unsalted butter, softened

about 250 g/9 oz icing sugar (see method)

1 tbsp milk

1 tsp vanilla extract

pinch of salt

green food colouring

1. Preheat the oven to 180°C/350°F/Gas Mark 4 and line a 12-hole cupcake tin with paper cases.

2. Sift together the flour, baking powder and salt in a bowl. Put the butter and caster sugar into a separate bowl and beat until pale and fluffy. Add the vanilla extract, then add the eggs, one at a time, beating after each addition. Add half of the flour mixture and the milk and beat until incorporated. Add the remaining flour mixture and mix. Add several drops of food colouring and beat until evenly combined. Gradually add more colouring until a vibrant pink is achieved. Stir in the chocolate chips.

3. Spoon the batter into the paper cases and bake in the preheated oven for 20 minutes, until risen and a cocktail stick inserted into the centre of a cupcake comes out clean. Leave to cool in the tin for 1–2 minutes, then transfer to a wire rack to cool completely.

4. To make the frosting, put the butter, icing sugar, milk, vanilla extract and salt into a bowl and beat with an electric mixer until well combined. Add more icing sugar, if necessary, to achieve a piping consistency. Add several drops of food colouring and beat until evenly incorporated. Gradually add more colouring until a dark green colour is achieved. Transfer the frosting to a piping bag fitted with a star-shaped tip and pipe onto the cupcakes. Serve.

Top tip

Replace the vanilla extract in the batter and the frosting with watermelon candy flavouring for the full effect.

2

3

4

Hamburger Cupcakes

makes 12
brownie burgers

60 g/2¼ oz plain flour

50 g/1¾ oz cocoa powder

⅛ tsp baking powder

⅛ tsp salt

60 g/2¼ oz unsalted butter, softened, plus extra for greasing

150 g/5½ oz caster sugar

1 tsp vanilla extract

1 large egg

cupcake buns

190 g/6¾ oz plain flour

1½ tsp baking powder

¼ tsp salt

115 g/4 oz unsalted butter, softened, plus extra for greasing

200 g/7 oz caster sugar

2 tsp vanilla extract

2 large eggs

125 ml/4 fl oz milk

frosting

115 g/4 oz unsalted butter, softened

about 250 g/9 oz icing sugar (see method)

1 tbsp milk

1 tsp vanilla extract

pinch of salt

red food colouring

yellow food colouring

1. Preheat the oven to 180°C/350°F/Gas Mark 4 and grease two 12-hole cupcake tins.

2. To make the brownie burgers, sift together the flour, cocoa powder, baking powder and salt in a bowl. Put the butter and caster sugar into a separate bowl and beat until pale and fluffy. Add the vanilla extract, then beat in the egg. Gradually add the flour mixture, beating until well combined. Spoon the batter into the cases in one of the prepared tins. Bake in the preheated oven for 20 minutes, or until a cocktail stick inserted into the centre of a brownie comes out clean. Leave to cool in the tin for 5 minutes, then carefully transfer to a wire rack to cool completely (do not switch off the oven). Once cooled, trim each brownie into a perfect round using a 5-cm/2-inch round cutter.

3. To make the cupcake buns, sift together the flour, baking powder and salt in a bowl. Put the butter and caster sugar into a separate bowl and beat until pale and fluffy. Add the vanilla extract, then add the eggs, one at a time, beating after each addition. Add half of the flour mixture and the milk and beat until incorporated. Add the remaining flour mixture and mix.

4. Spoon the batter into the remaining prepared tin and bake for 20 minutes, until risen and a cocktail stick inserted into the centre of a cupcake comes out clean. Leave to cool in the tin for 1–2 minutes, then transfer to a wire rack to cool completely.

to decorate

green food colouring

75 g/2¾ oz desiccated coconut

clear honey

sesame seeds

5. To make the frosting, put the butter, icing sugar, milk, vanilla extract and salt into a bowl and beat until well combined. Add more icing sugar, if necessary, to achieve a piping consistency. Divide the frosting between two bowls. Add several drops of red food colouring to one bowl and beat until evenly combined – this will be tomato ketchup. Add a few drops of yellow food colouring to the second bowl and beat until evenly combined – this will be mustard. Transfer the frostings to small squeezy bottles or piping bags fitted with small round tips.

6. To make the lettuce to decorate, add a couple of drops of green food colouring to the coconut and toss until the coconut is evenly coloured.

7. To serve, slice the cupcakes in half horizontally to create the two halves of a burger bun. Place a brownie burger on top of half of the bun slices. Pipe the red and yellow frostings onto the brownie burgers and top with some of the coconut lettuce. Place the remaining halves of the cupcake buns on top of each burger and brush with a thin layer of honey. Sprinkle sesame seeds over the tops of the buns. Serve.

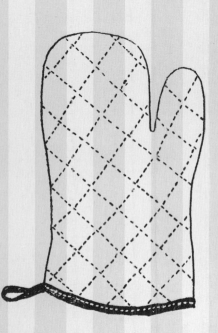

2

6

7

7

Top tip

Serve these moreish little hamburgers
with 'chips' made from vanilla sponge
cake, sliced and then rolled in a little
caster sugar.

Cupcake Shooters

makes 16

150 g/5½ oz self-raising flour

55 g/2 oz ground almonds

175 g/6 oz unsalted butter, softened

175 g/6 oz caster sugar

1 tsp vanilla extract

3 eggs, lightly beaten

frosting

115 g/8 oz unsalted butter, softened

about 175 g/6 oz icing sugar (see method)

1 tbsp double cream

1. Preheat the oven to 180°C/350°F/Gas Mark 4 and line an 8-hole cupcake tin with paper cases.

2. Sift together the flour and ground almonds in a bowl. Put the butter and caster sugar into a separate bowl and beat until pale and fluffy. Add the vanilla extract, then add the eggs, one at a time, beating after each addition. Add half of the flour mixture and beat until incorporated. Add the remaining flour mixture and mix.

3. Spoon the batter into the paper cases and bake in the preheated oven for 20 minutes, until risen and golden. Leave to cool in the tin for 1–2 minutes, then transfer to a wire rack to cool completely.

4. To make the frosting, put the butter, icing sugar and cream into a bowl and beat with an electric mixer until well combined. Add more icing sugar, if necessary, to achieve a piping consistency. Transfer the frosting to a piping bag fitted with a small star-shaped tip.

5. Crumble the cooled cupcakes into a bowl. Transfer to 16 clear shot glasses, filling each three-quarters full. Pipe the frosting onto the cake crumbs and serve.

Top tip

This recipe is for basic
vanilla-flavoured shooters, but you
could use any cake and frosting
combination you like!

Hot Choc Cupcakes

makes 12

60 g/2¼ oz plain flour

40 g/1½ oz cocoa powder

¾ tsp baking powder

⅛ tsp salt

60 g/2¼ oz unsalted butter, softened, plus extra for greasing

100 g/3½ oz caster sugar

1 tsp vanilla extract

1 large egg

4 tbsp double cream

350 g/12 oz white chocolate, broken into pieces

36 mini marshmallows, to decorate

chocolate ganache

225 g/8 oz plain chocolate, chopped

125 ml/4 fl oz double cream

1 tbsp golden syrup

frosting

1 large egg white

50 g/1¾ oz granulated sugar

150 g/5½ oz unsalted butter, softened

1 tsp vanilla extract

1. Preheat the oven to 180°C/350°C/Gas Mark 4 and lightly grease a 12-hole mini cupcake tin.

2. Sift together the flour, cocoa powder, baking powder and salt in a bowl. Put the butter and caster sugar into a separate bowl and beat until pale and fluffy. Add the vanilla extract, then add the egg and beat until combined. Add half of the flour mixture and the cream and beat until incorporated. Add the remaining flour mixture and mix.

3. Spoon the batter into the prepared tin and bake in the preheated oven for 15 minutes, until risen and a cocktail stick inserted into the centre of a mini cupcake comes out clean. Leave to cool in the tin for 1–2 minutes, then transfer to a wire rack to cool completely.

4. To make the white chocolate cups, place the white chocolate in a heatproof bowl set over a saucepan of gently simmering water and stir until the chocolate has completed melted.

5. Spoon a little of the melted chocolate into a paper cup (the cup must be big enough to hold one of your mini cupcakes). Slowly turn the cup and use the back of the spoon to coat white chocolate on the base and about halfway up the inside of the cup. Continue turning until the chocolate begins to set, which may take a few minutes. Place in the refrigerator to set completely. Repeat until you have 12 cups. Once the chocolate has set, gently pop the chocolate cups out of the paper cups, carefully tearing away the paper if necessary. Store in the refrigerator until ready to use.

6. To make the chocolate ganache, place the chocolate and cream in a heatproof bowl set over a saucepan of gently simmering water and whisk until the chocolate has completely melted. Stir in the golden syrup. Remove from the heat and set aside to cool and thicken slightly.

7. To make the frosting, put the egg white and granulated sugar in a heatproof bowl set over a saucepan of gently simmering water and whisk until the sugar has completely dissolved. Remove from the heat and whisk the mixture for 4–5 minutes. Add the butter, 2 tablespoons at a time, and continue to beat until it holds stiff peaks. Add the vanilla extract and beat until incorporated. Spoon the frosting into a piping bag fitted with a star-shaped tip.

8. Place a cupcake in each white chocolate cup. Spoon chocolate ganache over the top to cover each cupcake completely. Pipe frosting onto the ganache to look like a dollop of whipped cream, then place 3 mini marshmallows on top of each.

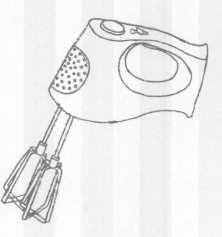

Top tip

Forgo the white chocolate cup and instead serve the mini muffins in a teacup, topped with the chocolate ganache.

Ice Cream Sundae Cupcakes

makes 18

vanilla & strawberry cupcakes

190 g/6¾ oz plain flour

1½ tsp baking powder

¼ tsp salt

115 g/4 oz unsalted butter, softened

200 g/7 oz caster sugar

2 tsp vanilla extract

2 large eggs

125 ml/4 fl oz milk

pink food colouring

85 g/3 oz fresh strawberries, diced

chocolate cupcakes

60 g/2¼ oz plain flour

50 g/1¾ oz cocoa powder

¾ tsp baking powder

⅛ tsp salt

60 g/2¼ oz unsalted butter, softened

100 g/3½ oz caster sugar

1 tsp vanilla extract

1 large egg

4 tbsp double cream

frosting

3 large egg whites

150 g/5½ oz granulated sugar

225 g/8 oz unsalted butter, softened

1 tsp vanilla extract

pinch of salt

1. Preheat the oven to 180°C/350°F/Gas Mark 4 and line a 12-hole cupcake tin with paper cases.

2. To make the vanilla cupcakes, sift together the flour, baking powder and salt in a bowl. Put the butter and caster sugar into a separate bowl and beat until pale and fluffy. Add the vanilla extract, then add the eggs, one at a time, beating after each addition. Add half of the flour mixture and the milk and beat until incorporated. Add the remaining flour mixture and mix.

3. Spoon half of the batter into 6 of the paper cases.

4. To make the strawberry cupcakes, add a few drops of food colouring to the remaining batter and mix until incorporated. Add the strawberries and stir. Spoon the batter into the 6 remaining paper cases.

5. Bake in the preheated oven for about 20 minutes, until risen and a cocktail stick inserted into the centre of a cupcake comes out clean. Leave to cool in the tin for 1–2 minutes, then transfer to a wire rack to cool completely (do not switch off the oven).

6. Put 6 paper cases into another 12-hole cupcake tin.

7. To make the chocolate cupcakes, sift together the flour, cocoa powder, baking powder and salt in a bowl. Put the butter and caster sugar into a separate bowl and beat until pale and fluffy. Add the vanilla extract, then add the egg and beat until combined. Add half of the flour mixture and the cream and beat until incorporated. Add the remaining flour mixture and mix.

chocolate sauce

55 g/2 oz plain chocolate, broken into pieces

3 tbsp double cream

15 g/½ oz unsalted butter

pinch of salt

to fill and decorate

450 ml/16 fl oz ice cream, softened

60 g/2¼ oz chopped mixed nuts

18 maraschino cherries

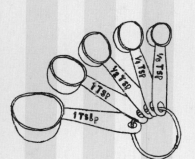

8. Spoon the batter into the paper cases and bake in the preheated oven for 20 minutes, until risen and a cocktail stick inserted into the centre of a cupcake comes out clean. Leave to cool in the tin for 1–2 minutes, then transfer to a wire rack to cool completely.

9. To fill the cupcake, use an apple corer to remove the centre of the cupcakes. Spoon the ice cream into the holes. Transfer the cupcakes to the freezer until you are ready to frost them.

10. To make the frosting, put the egg whites and granulated sugar in a heatproof bowl set over a saucepan of gently simmering water and whisk until the sugar has completely dissolved. Remove from the heat and whisk the mixture for 4–5 minutes. Add the butter, 2 tablespoons at a time, and continue to beat until it holds stiff peaks. Add the vanilla extract and salt and beat until just combined. Spoon the frosting into a piping bag fitted with a star-shaped tip.

11. To make the chocolate sauce, put the chocolate, cream, butter and salt into a heatproof bowl set over a saucepan of gently simmering water and stir until the chocolate has completely melted. Set aside to cool for at least 15 minutes.

12. Pipe the frosting onto the chilled, filled cupcakes. To decorate, drizzle the chocolate sauce over the top and sprinkle with chopped nuts. Place a cherry on each cupcake.

9

Top tip

As an alternative to frosting, scoop softened ice cream into a piping bag and pipe on top of the chilled cupcakes before serving.

9

12

Little Sprigs Cupcakes

makes 12

125 g/4½ oz plain flour

60 g/2¼ oz cocoa powder

1 tsp baking powder

¼ tsp salt

115 g/4 oz unsalted butter, softened

200 g/7 oz caster sugar

2 tsp vanilla extract

2 large eggs

125 ml/4 fl oz double cream

frosting

115 g/4 oz unsalted butter, softened

about 190 g/6¾ oz icing sugar (see method)

40 g/1½ oz cocoa powder

1 tbsp milk

¼ tsp salt

1 tsp vanilla extract

to decorate

115 g/4 oz chocolate wafer biscuits, crushed

225 g/8 oz green candy melts

1. Preheat the oven to 180°C/350°F/Gas Mark 4 and line a 12-hole cupcake tin with paper cases.

2. Sift together the flour, cocoa powder, baking powder and salt in a bowl. Put the butter and caster sugar into a separate bowl and beat until pale and fluffy. Add the vanilla extract, then add the eggs, one at a time, beating after each addition. Add half of the flour mixture and the cream and beat until incorporated. Add the remaining flour mixture and mix.

3. Spoon the batter into the paper cases and bake in the preheated oven for 20 minutes, until risen and a cocktail stick inserted into the centre of a cupcake comes out clean. Leave to cool in the tin for 1–2 minutes, then transfer to a wire rack to cool completely.

4. To make the frosting, put the butter, icing sugar, cocoa powder, milk, salt and vanilla extract into a bowl and beat with an electric mixer until smooth. Add more icing sugar if necessary, to achieve a piping consistency.

5. Using a palette knife, spread the frosting on top of the cupcakes. To decorate, place the biscuit crumbs in a shallow dish and press the top of each frosted cupcake into them, to coat.

6. Melt the candy melts according to the packet instructions and transfer to a piping bag fitted with a small, round tip. Pipe 12 plant shapes onto a sheet of baking paper. Transfer to the refrigerator to set. To serve, insert a plant 'sprig' in the top of each cupcake.

Top tip

Alternatively, use coloured ready-to-roll fondant icing to form the plants sprouting from the top of the cupcakes.

Little Lion Cupcakes

makes 12

190 g/6¾ oz plain flour

1½ tsp baking powder

¼ tsp salt

115 g/4 oz unsalted butter, softened

200 g/7 oz caster sugar

2 tsp vanilla extract

2 large eggs

125 ml/4 fl oz milk

250 g/9 oz yellow ready-to-roll fondant icing and black writing icing, to decorate

frosting

225 g/8 oz unsalted butter, softened

about 425 g/15 oz icing sugar (see method)

2 tbsp milk

2 tsp vanilla extract

1 tsp ground cinnamon

orange food colouring

1. Preheat the oven to 180°C/350°F/Gas Mark 4 and line a 12-hole cupcake tin with paper cases.

2. Sift together the flour, baking powder and salt in a bowl. Put the butter and caster sugar into a separate bowl and beat until pale and fluffy. Add the vanilla extract, then add the eggs, one at a time, beating after each addition. Add half of the flour mixture and the milk and beat until incorporated. Add the remaining flour mixture and mix.

3. Spoon the batter into the paper cases and bake in the preheated oven for 20 minutes, until risen and golden. Leave to cool in the tin for 1–2 minutes, then transfer to a wire rack to cool completely.

4. To make the frosting, put the butter, icing sugar, milk, vanilla extract, cinnamon and a few drops of orange food colouring into a bowl and beat with an electric mixer until well combined. Add more icing sugar, if necessary, to achieve a piping consistency.

5. Spoon the frosting into a piping bag fitted with a star-shaped tip. Pipe wiggly lines of frosting all over the tops of the cupcakes, pulling the ends away from the cake to give a manelike appearance.

6. For the decoration, divide the fondant icing into 12 pieces. Take one of these pieces and pinch off four small pieces of the fondant and set aside. Shape the remaining fondant into a heart shape and position in the middle of a frosted cupcake. Form the reserved pieces into flattened rounds, and position two on top of the frosting (these are the "ears") and two on top of the fondant icing shape (these are the "cheeks").

7. Using a toothpick, prick the "cheeks" all over, to look like whiskers. Using the writing icing, add two eyes, a nose and a mouth. Let set.

8. Repeat with the remaining fondant icing and the remaining cupcakes. Serve.

Flamingo Cupcakes

makes 12

190 g/6¾ oz plain flour

1½ tsp baking powder

¼ tsp salt

115 g/4 oz unsalted butter, softened

200 g/7 oz caster sugar

2 tsp vanilla extract

2 large eggs

125 ml/4 fl oz milk

frosting

115 g/4 oz unsalted butter, softened

about 250 g/9 oz icing sugar (see method)

1 tbsp milk

1 tsp vanilla extract

pinch of salt

blue food colouring

to decorate

pink food colouring

225 g/8 oz ready-made gum paste, at room temperature

cornflour, for dusting

black edible-ink marker

piping gel

pink sugar crystals

1. To make the flamingo decorations, add several drops of food colouring to the gum paste and knead, on a surface lightly dusted with cornflour, until the colour is evenly distributed. Gradually add more colouring until a bright pink colour is achieved.

2. Divide the gum paste into 3 pieces and roll 1 piece out to a thickness of 2.5 mm/⅛ inch. Use a 6-cm/2½-inch flamingo-shaped cookie cutter to cut out 4 flamingos. Repeat with the remaining gum paste. Set aside to dry overnight.

3. When the gum paste has hardened, use a black edible-ink marker to draw an eye and beak on each flamingo. Next, use a small brush to paint a thin layer of piping gel in a wing shape on to the side of each. Sprinkle with pink sugar crystals and set aside to dry.

4. Preheat the oven to 180°C/350°F/Gas Mark 4 and line a 12-hole cupcake tin with paper cases.

5. Sift together the flour, baking powder and salt in a bowl. Put the butter and caster sugar into a separate bowl and beat until pale and fluffy. Add the vanilla extract, then add the eggs, one at a time, beating after each addition. Add half of the flour mixture and the milk and beat until incorporated. Add the remaining flour mixture and mix.

6. Spoon the batter into the paper cases and bake in the preheated oven for 20 minutes, until risen and a cocktail stick inserted into the centre of a cupcake comes out clean. Leave to cool in the tin for 1–2 minutes, then transfer to a wire rack to cool completely.

7. To make the frosting, put the butter, icing sugar, milk, vanilla extract and salt into a bowl and beat with an electric mixer until well combined. Add more icing sugar, if necessary, to achieve a piping consistency. Add a few drops of blue food colouring and beat until it is evenly incorporated. Gradually add more colouring until the desired colour is achieved. Spoon the frosting into a piping bag fitted with a star-shaped tip.

8. Pipe the frosting onto the cupcakes and stand a flamingo in the centre of each. Serve.

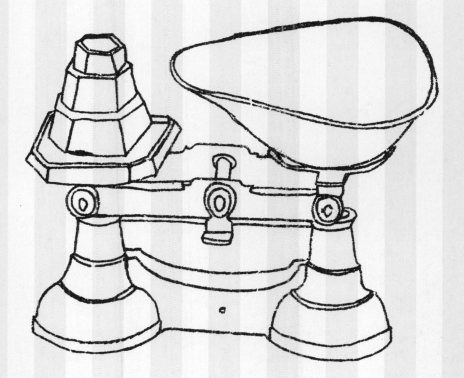

Top tip

If the gum paste flamingos are too delicate to stand, use a little ready-to-roll fondant icing, or more gum paste to attach a cocktail stick to the back of the leg.

Belly-up Bear Cupcakes

makes 12

190 g/6¾ oz plain flour

1½ tsp baking powder

¼ tsp salt

115 g/4 oz unsalted butter, softened

200 g/7 oz soft light brown sugar

2 tsp coconut extract

2 large eggs

125 ml/4 fl oz unsweetened coconut milk

frosting

2 large egg whites

60 g/2¼ oz granulated sugar

150 g/5½ oz unsalted butter, softened

1 tsp coconut extract

2 tbsp coconut cream

pinch of salt

to decorate

12 white round marshmallows

225 g/8 oz desiccated coconut

250 g/9 oz white ready-to-roll fondant icing

12 mini candy-coated chocolates

brown writing icing

1. Preheat the oven to 180°C/350°F/Gas Mark 4 and line a 12-hole cupcake tin with paper cases.

2. Sift together the flour, baking powder and salt in a bowl. Put the butter and brown sugar into a separate bowl and beat until pale and fluffy. Add the coconut extract, then add the eggs, one at a time, beating between each addition, until well incorporated. Add half of the flour mixture and the coconut milk and beat until incorporated. Add the remaining flour mixture and mix.

3. Spoon the batter into the paper cases and bake in the preheated oven for 20 minutes, until risen and golden. Leave to cool in the tin for 1–2 minutes, then transfer to a wire rack to cool completely.

4. To make the frosting, put the egg whites and granulated sugar in a heatproof bowl set over a saucepan of gently simmering water and whisk until the sugar has completely dissolved. Remove from the heat and whisk the mixture for 4–5 minutes, until it holds stiff peaks. Add the butter, 2 tablespoons at a time, and continue to beat until it holds stiff peaks. Add the coconut extract, coconut cream and salt, and beat until just combined.

5. Using a palette knife, spread the frosting on top of the cupcakes. Place a round marshmallow at the top edge of each cupcake. Spread frosting over and around the marshmallow, filling in the gap where the marshmallow meets the cupcake.

6. Put the desiccated coconut in a shallow bowl. Hold a frosted cupcake over the bowl and sprinkle the coconut over it, pressing it in as needed to make sure it sticks to the cupcake and all over the head.

7. For the decoration, divide the fondant icing into 12 pieces. Take one of these pieces and divide into six. Shape two of these into ovals for the "bottom paws" and two into rounds for the "top paws". Press in place on the sides of the cupcake. Use one of the remaining pieces of fondant to create the "face" and press in place on the front of the cupcake. Divide the last remaining piece of fondant in two to create the "ears" and press these in place on top of the cupcake.

8. Position a candy-coated chocolate in place on the face, to create a "nose". Then use the writing icing to add two eyes, a mouth, and details to the paws. Let set.

9. Repeat with the remaining fondant icing and the remaining cupcakes. Serve.

3

5

6

Top tip

Alternatively, omit the coconut over the frosting, and instead dip the bear in white candy melts to coat (simply chill in the freezer before).

Cactus Cupcakes

makes 12

190 g/6¾ oz plain flour

1½ tsp baking powder

¼ tsp salt

115 g/4 oz unsalted butter, softened

200 g/7 oz caster sugar

2 tsp vanilla extract

2 large eggs

finely grated rind and juice of
1 lime

125 ml/4 fl oz milk

frosting

115 g/4 oz unsalted butter, softened

about 250 g/9 oz icing sugar
(see method)

1 tbsp lime juice

1 tsp finely grated lime rind

to decorate

green food colouring

350 g/12 oz ready-made gum paste

cornflour, for dusting

pink food colouring

piping gel

green sugar crystals

115 g/4 oz digestive biscuits,
crushed

1. To make the decorations, add a few drops of green food colouring to 280 g/10 oz of gum paste and knead on a work surface lightly dusted with cornflour until evenly incorporated. Roll out to about 2.5 mm/⅛inch thick and cut out 12 cacti. Set aside to dry. Colour the remaining gum paste with pink food colouring and roll out to 2.5 mm/⅛ inch thick. Cut out about 60 flowers and set aside to dry.

2. Once hardened, use a small brush to coat the cacti with piping gel. Attach the flowers and then sprinkle over the sugar crystals. Set aside.

3. Preheat the oven to 180°C/350°F/Gas Mark 4 and line a 12-hole cupcake tin with paper cases.

4. Sift together the flour, baking powder and salt in a bowl. Put the butter and caster sugar into a separate bowl and beat until pale and fluffy. Add the vanilla extract, then add the eggs, one at a time, beating after each addition. Add the lime rind and juice and beat until incorporated. Add half of the flour mixture and the milk and beat until incorporated. Add the remaining flour mixture and mix.

5. Spoon the batter into the paper cases and bake in the preheated oven for 20 minutes, until risen and golden. Leave to cool in the tin for 1–2 minutes, then transfer to a wire rack to cool completely.

6. To make the frosting, put the butter, icing sugar, lime juice and rind into a bowl and beat with an electric mixer until well combined. Add more icing sugar, if necessary, to achieve a piping consistency.

7. Using a palette knife, spread the frosting evenly on top of the cupcakes. Sprinkle with the biscuit crumbs and then insert a cactus on top of each cupcake.

Fun & Frosted
Chapter 3

CHAPTER 4
SCARY
CUTE

6

7

9

Top tip

Be sure to use chocolate
coating. Unlike standard
chocolate, it provides a nice,
crunchy finish.

6

7

8

Top tip

Impress guests at a Halloween party with an extra hand-made detail — make the worms out of ready-to-roll fondant icing too.

Neon Cupcakes

makes 12

190 g/6¾ oz plain flour

1½ tsp baking powder

¼ tsp salt

115 g/4 oz unsalted butter, softened

200 g/7 oz caster sugar

2 tsp vanilla extract

2 large eggs

125 ml/4 fl oz milk

350 g/12 oz white chocolate coating, to decorate

frosting

115 g/4 oz unsalted butter, softened

about 250 g/9 oz icing sugar (see method)

1 tbsp milk

1 tsp vanilla extract

pinch of salt

neon food colouring, 3 different colours

1. Preheat the oven to 180°C/350°F/Gas Mark 4. Line 2 baking sheets with baking paper and line a 12-hole cupcake tin with paper cases.

2. Sift together the flour, baking powder and salt in a bowl. Put the butter and caster sugar into a separate bowl and beat until pale and fluffy. Add the vanilla extract, then add the eggs, one at a time, beating after each addition. Add half of the flour mixture and the milk and beat until incorporated. Add the remaining flour mixture and mix.

3. Spoon the batter into the paper cases and bake in the preheated oven for 20 minutes, until risen and golden. Leave to cool in the tin for 1–2 minutes, then transfer to a wire rack to cool completely.

4. To make the frosting, put the butter, icing sugar, milk, vanilla extract and salt into a bowl and beat with an electric mixer until well combined. Add more icing sugar, if necessary, to achieve a piping consistency. Divide the frosting between 3 bowls and colour each with a different food colouring. Spoon each frosting into a piping bag fitted with a star-shaped tip. Refrigerate until ready to use.

5. To make the spider's webs, put the chocolate coating in a heatproof bowl set over a saucepan of gently simmering water and whisk until the chocolate has completely melted. Transfer to a piping bag fitted with a small round tip and pipe onto the prepared baking sheets, in a spider's web shape. Repeat to make 12 webs. Place in the refrigerator and chill until the chocolate has set.

6. Pipe the frosting onto the cupcakes. To serve, top each cupcake with a spider's web.

FLOUR

for good baking

1.5 kg

5

6

6

Ghost Cupcakes

makes 6

140 g/5 oz plain flour

2 tsp ground mixed spice

¾ tsp bicarbonate of soda

85 g/3 oz unsalted butter, softened

85 g/3 oz dark muscovado sugar

1 tbsp black treacle

2 large eggs

frosting

85 g/3 oz unsalted butter, softened

1 tbsp dulce de leche

about 175 g/6 oz icing sugar (see method)

to decorate

350 g/12 oz white ready-to-roll fondant icing

icing sugar, for dusting

black writing icing

1. Preheat the oven to 180°C/350°F/Gas Mark 4. Line a 12-hole cupcake tin with paper cases and line a 6-hole mini cupcake tin with paper cases.

2. Sift together the flour, mixed spice and bicarbonate of soda into a bowl. Put the butter, sugar and treacle into a separate bowl and beat until fluffy. Then add the eggs, one at a time, beating after each addition. Add half of the flour mixture and beat until incorporated. Add the remaining flour mixture and mix.

3. Spoon the batter into the 18 paper cases. Bake the mini cupcakes in the preheated oven for 10 minutes and the standard cupcakes for 20 minutes, until risen and golden. Leave to cool in the tin for 1–2 minutes, then transfer to a wire rack to cool completely.

4. To make the frosting, put the butter, dulce de leche and icing sugar into a bowl and beat with an electric mixer until well combined. Add more icing sugar, if necessary, to achieve a piping consistency.

5. To assemble and decorate, remove the paper cases from 6 of the standard cupcakes and all of the mini cupcake. Spread a layer of frosting over the top of the remaining cupcakes. Top each with an upturned standard cupcake, and then an upturned mini cupcake. Spread frosting over the stacked cakes, then transfer to the refrigerator to chill for 30 minutes.

6. Take 50 g/1¾ oz of white fondant icing and roll into 6 small balls. Place one on top of each of the cakes. Divide the remaining fondant into 6 pieces and roll out each piece on a surface dusted with icing sugar to a 14-cm/5½-inch round. Drape over the cupcakes and then use the black writing icing to pipe eyes onto the cake. Serve.

Top tip

Cut and then drape the fondant icing
on one cupcake at a time — this will
prevent it from drying out and
becoming brittle.

Zombie Cupcakes

makes 12

125 g/4½ oz plain flour

60 g/2¼ oz cocoa powder

1½ tsp baking powder

¼ tsp salt

115 g/4 oz unsalted butter, softened

200 g/7 oz caster sugar

2 tsp vanilla extract

2 large eggs

125 ml/4 fl oz double cream

ganache

350 g/12 oz plain chocolate, chopped

125 ml/4 fl oz double cream

4 tsp golden syrup

to decorate

green food colouring

85 g/3 oz white ready-to-roll fondant icing

175 g/6 oz plain chocolate-flavoured cake covering, broken into pieces

white writing icing

125 g/4½ oz chocolate wafer biscuits, crushed

1. To make the zombie hand decorations, lay out a large sheet of baking paper. Add a small drop of green food colouring to the fondant icing and knead until the colour is evenly distributed. Pinch off a 2 cm/¾ inch ball of icing and flatten into a rectangle, about 6 x 2.5 cm/2½ x 1 inch. Using a small, sharp paring knife, cut out 4 fingers and a thumb for the hand and an arm extending about 4 cm/1½ inches below the hand. Round the edges using the tips of your fingers and place on the baking paper. Repeat until you have 12 hands. Set aside and leave to dry, uncovered, overnight.

2. Preheat the oven to 180°C/350°F/Gas Mark 4 and line a 12-hole cupcake tin with paper cases.

3. Sift together the flour, cocoa powder, baking powder and salt in a bowl. Put the butter and caster sugar into a separate bowl and beat until pale and fluffy. Add the vanilla extract, then add the eggs, one at a time, beating after each addition. Add half of the flour mixture and the cream and beat until incorporated. Add the remaining flour mixture and mix.

4. Spoon the batter into the paper cases and bake in the preheated oven for 20 minutes, until risen and a cocktail stick inserted into the centre of a cupcake comes out clean. Leave to cool in the tin for 1–2 minutes, then transfer to a wire rack to cool completely.

5. To make the tombstones to decorate, place the chocolate-flavoured cake covering in a heatproof bowl set over a saucepan of gently simmering water and stir until the chocolate has completely melted.

6. Draw 12 tombstone shapes (a rectangle with a rounded top, about 6 x 4 cm/ 2½ x 1½ inches) on a large piece of baking paper. Turn the paper over so that the drawings are on the bottom (you should be able to see it through the paper) and lay the paper on a baking sheet. Using a small spoon, drop a small amount of the melted chocolate onto one of the tombstone images and, using the back of the spoon, spread it out to fill the image, so that you have a thin, tombstone-shaped portion of chocolate. Repeat until you have 12 tombstones. Place the baking sheet in the refrigerator to chill for about 10 minutes. When the chocolate has hardened, remove the tray from the refrigerator and write the letters 'RIP' on each tombstone using the white writing icing.

7. To make the ganache, combine the chocolate and cream in a heatproof bowl set over a saucepan of gently simmering water and whisk until the chocolate has completely melted. Stir in the golden syrup until it is fully incorporated. Remove from the heat and set aside to cool and thicken slightly.

8. When the cupcakes are completely cool, spoon the ganache onto them, spreading it out using the back of the spoon so that it evenly coats the tops of the cupcakes. Sprinkle the crushed wafer biscuits over the top.

9. Place one tombstone in the top of each cupcake, towards the back. Stick a zombie hand into the middle of the cupcake so that it looks as if the hand is coming up out of the 'grave'. Serve the cupcakes at room temperature.

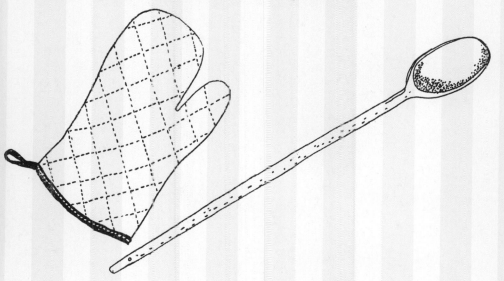

Pumpkin Cupcakes

makes 12

190 g/6¾ oz plain flour

1½ tsp baking powder

¾ tsp ground cinnamon

¾ tsp ground ginger

¼ tsp salt

⅛ tsp ground nutmeg

⅛ tsp ground allspice

115 g/4 oz unsalted butter, softened

100 g/3½ oz caster sugar

100 g/3½ oz soft light brown sugar

1 tsp vanilla extract

2 large eggs

175 g/6 oz canned unsweetened pumpkin purée

frosting

115 g/4 oz unsalted butter, softened

about 250 g/9 oz icing sugar (see method)

1 tbsp milk

1 tsp vanilla extract

1 tsp ground cinnamon

pinch of salt

red food colouring

yellow food colouring

to decorate

orange sugar crystals

55 g/2 oz green ready-to-roll fondant icing

1. Preheat the oven to 180°C/350°F/Gas Mark 4 and line a 12-hole cupcake tin with paper cases.

2. Sift together the flour, baking powder, cinnamon, ginger, salt, nutmeg and allspice in a bowl. Put the butter, caster sugar and brown sugar into a separate bowl and beat until pale and fluffy. Add the vanilla extract, then add the eggs, one at a time, beating after each addition. Add half of the flour mixture and the pumpkin purée and beat until incorporated. Add the remaining flour mixture and mix.

3. Spoon the batter into the paper cases and bake in the preheated oven for 20 minutes, until risen and golden. Leave to cool in the tin for 1–2 minutes, then transfer to a wire rack to cool completely.

4. To make the frosting, put the butter, icing sugar, milk, vanilla extract, cinnamon and salt into a bowl and beat with an electric mixer until well combined. Add more icing sugar, if necessary, to achieve a piping consistency. Add a few drops of red and yellow food colouring and beat until evenly incorporated. Add more of either or both colours until the desired shade of orange is achieved.

5. Place a generous tablespoonful of orange frosting on top of each cupcake. Use a palette knife to spread it onto the cupcake, building a rounded dome on top. Push a small indent into the top of the frosting. To decorate, place the sugar crystals in a shallow bowl and press the top of each cupcake into the crystals to coat.

6. Pinch off a small piece of the fondant and shape it into a 2.5 cm/1 inch stem. Repeat to make 12 in total. To serve, insert the stems into the indents in the frosting.

Top tip
The pumpkin cupcakes are also delicious topped with a cream cheese frosting, like the one on page 60.

5

5

6

Toadstool Cupcakes

makes 12

190 g/6¾ oz plain flour

1½ tsp baking powder

¼ tsp salt

115 g/4 oz unsalted butter, softened

200 g/7 oz caster sugar

2 tsp vanilla extract

2 large eggs

125 ml/4 fl oz milk

85 g/3 oz white ready-to-roll fondant icing, to decorate

icing sugar, for dusting

frosting

115 g/4 oz unsalted butter, softened

about 250 g/9 oz icing sugar (see method)

1 tbsp milk

1 tsp vanilla extract

pinch of salt

red food colouring

1. Preheat the oven to 180°C/350°F/Gas Mark 4 and line a 12-hole cupcake tin with paper cases.

2. Sift together the flour, baking powder and salt in a bowl. Put the butter and caster sugar into a separate bowl and beat until pale and fluffy. Add the vanilla extract, then add the eggs, one at a time, beating after each addition. Add half of the flour mixture and the milk and beat until incorporated. Add the remaining flour mixture and mix.

3. Spoon the batter into the paper cases and bake in the preheated oven for 20 minutes, until risen and golden. Leave to cool in the tin for 1–2 minutes, then transfer to a wire rack to cool completely.

4. To make the frosting, put the butter, icing sugar, milk, vanilla extract and salt into a bowl and beat until well combined. Add more icing sugar, if necessary, to achieve a piping consistency. Add several drops of red food colouring and beat until evenly incorporated. Gradually add more colouring until a bright red colour is achieved.

5. Roll out the fondant icing on a surface dusted with icing sugar and use a 5-mm/¼-inch round cutter to cut out about 60 dots.

6. Remove the cupcakes from the paper cases. Carefully cut off the tops of the cupcakes using a serrated knife and reserve. Use a 4-cm/1½-inch round cutter to cut the remaining cupcakes into stems for the mushrooms. Discard the trimmings. Spread frosting on top of each stem and place the reserved cupcake tops on top to create the mushroom caps. Spread frosting over the caps of the mushrooms, and position the white dots on top.

5

6

6

Octopus Cupcakes

makes 12

190 g/6¾ oz plain flour

1½ tsp baking powder

¼ tsp salt

115 g/4 oz unsalted butter, softened

200 g/7 oz caster sugar

2 tsp vanilla extract

2 large eggs

125 ml/4 fl oz milk

frosting

115 g/4 oz unsalted butter, softened

about 250 g/9 oz icing sugar (see method)

1 tbsp milk

1 tsp vanilla extract

pinch of salt

blue food colouring

to decorate

280 g/10 oz ready-made gum paste, at room temperature

cornflour, for dusting

blue food colouring

piping gel

24 small gum paste eyeballs

1. To make the octopus decorations, line a baking sheet with baking paper. Knead the gum paste on a board lightly dusted with cornflour until it is pliable. Add a few drops of food colouring and knead until the colour is evenly incorporated.

2. To make the legs, break off a 1-cm/½-inch ball of gum paste and roll it into a 7.5- x 0.25-cm/3- x ⅛-inch cylinder, rounded at one end. Place on the prepared baking sheet and repeat until you have 96 legs (8 for each cupcake).

3. To make the heads, break off a 15-mm/¾-inch piece of gum paste and roll it into a smooth ball. Lightly press onto a flat surface so that the base flattens. Place on the baking sheet with the legs. Repeat until you have 12 heads. Set aside to dry.

4. Preheat the oven to 180°C/350°F/Gas Mark 4 and line a 12-hole cupcake tin with blue paper cases.

5. Sift together the flour, baking powder and salt in a bowl. Put the butter and caster sugar into a separate bowl and beat until pale and fluffy. Add the vanilla extract, then add the eggs, one at a time, beating after each addition. Add half of the flour mixture and the milk and beat until incorporated. Add the remaining flour mixture and mix.

6. Spoon the batter into the paper cases and bake in the preheated oven for 20 minutes, until risen and golden. Leave to cool in the tin for 1–2 minutes, then transfer to a wire rack to cool completely.

7. To make the frosting, put the butter, icing sugar, milk, vanilla extract and salt into a bowl and beat with an electric mixer until well combined. Add more icing sugar, if necessary, to achieve a piping consistency. Add a few drops of blue food colouring and beat until evenly incorporated. Add more colouring until the mixture is the same colour as the gum paste shapes.

8. To finish the octopus heads, use a small brush to spread a thin layer of piping gel onto the back of each gum paste eyeball and place a pair of eyes on each head.

9. Use a palette knife to spread the frosting on top of the cupcakes in a thick layer. Place a head in the centre of each cupcake and place 8 legs around each one, pressing the ends into the frosting. Serve.

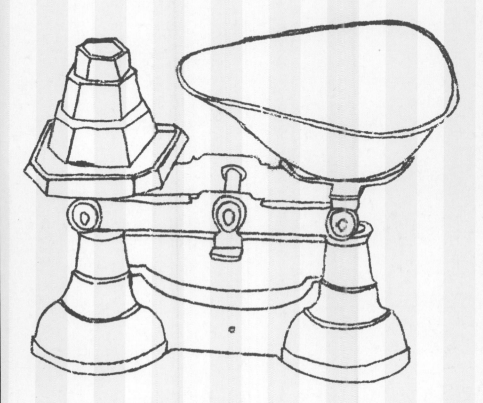

Top tip

Add further details to the head
and legs using a black
edible-ink marker pen or
writing icing.

Marshmallow Monster Cupcakes

makes 12

190 g/6¾ oz plain flour

1½ tsp baking powder

¼ tsp salt

115 g/4 oz unsalted butter, softened

200 g/7 oz caster sugar

2 tsp vanilla extract

2 large eggs

125 ml/4 fl oz milk

frosting

115 g/4 oz unsalted butter, softened

about 250 g/9 oz icing sugar (see method)

1 tbsp milk

1 tsp vanilla extract

pinch of salt

pink food colouring

blue food colouring

to decorate

piping gel

6 large round marshmallows, cut in half horizontally

12 mini marshmallows

12 large and 12 small gum paste eyeballs

55 g/2 oz white ready-to-roll fondant icing

1. Preheat the oven to 180°C/350°F/Gas Mark 4 and line a 12-hole cupcake tin with paper cases.

2. Sift together the flour, baking powder and salt in a bowl. Put the butter and caster sugar into a separate bowl and beat until pale and fluffy. Add the vanilla extract, then add the eggs, one at a time, beating after each addition. Add half of the flour mixture and the milk and beat until incorporated. Add the remaining flour mixture and mix.

3. Spoon the batter into the paper cases and bake in the preheated oven for 20 minutes, until risen and golden. Leave to cool in the tin for 1–2 minutes, then transfer to a wire rack to cool completely.

4. To make the frosting, put the butter, icing sugar, milk, vanilla extract and salt into a bowl and beat with an electric mixer until well combined. Add more icing sugar, if necessary, to achieve a piping consistency. Add a few drops of the pink food colouring and a few drops of the blue food colouring and beat until evenly incorporated. Spoon the frosting into a piping bag fitted with a star-shaped tip.

5. Using a brush, apply a light coat of piping gel to the top of the cupcakes and top with half a large marshmallow, on its side, and a small marshmallow next to it. Using more of the piping gel, attach a gum paste eyeball to the centre of each marshmallow.

6. Pipe frosting all over the top of the cupcakes, around the marshmallows. Roll out the fondant icing and cut out 24 small triangles, to use as teeth. Position 2 teeth on each cupcake underneath the eyes, and serve.

Top tip

Instead of marshmallows, try gummy
sweets or candy-coated chocolates —
simply adjust the colour of the frosting
to match.

Squished Witch Cupcakes

makes 12

190 g/6¾ oz plain flour

1½ tsp baking powder

¼ tsp salt

115 g/4 oz unsalted butter, softened

200 g/7 oz caster sugar

2 tsp vanilla extract

2 large eggs

125 ml/4 fl oz milk

finely grated rind and juice of 1 lime

green food colouring

250 g/9 oz lime curd

to decorate

280 g/10 oz white ready-made gum paste

cornflour, for dusting

black food colouring

red edible-ink marker

1. To make the witch legs for decoration, knead the gum paste on a board dusted with cornflour until it is a workable texture. Break off a 2.5-cm/1-inch piece and roll into a cylinder about 5 mm/¼ inch in diameter and about 13 cm/5 inches long. Cut in half to make 2 legs. Repeat until you have 24 legs.

2. Add several drops of black food colouring to the remaining gum paste and knead until the colour is evenly incorporated. Break off 1-cm/½-inch pieces and form them into boots with chunky heels and pointed toes. Attach one boot to the end of each leg by pressing the pieces together. Repeat until all of the legs have boots. Set aside to dry.

3. Preheat the oven to 180°C/350°F/Gas Mark 4 and line a 12-hole cupcake tin with paper cases.

4. Sift together the flour, baking powder and salt in a bowl. Put the butter and caster sugar into a separate bowl and beat until pale and fluffy. Add the vanilla extract, then add the eggs, one at a time, beating after each addition. Add half of the flour mixture and the milk and beat until incorporated. Add the remaining flour mixture and the lime rind and juice and mix.

5. Spoon the batter into the paper cases and bake in the preheated oven for 20 minutes, until risen and golden. Leave to cool in the tin for 1–2 minutes, then transfer to a wire rack to cool completely.

6. Stir a few drops of green food colouring into the lime curd and then spoon onto serving plates. Use the red edible-ink marker to draw stripes on the legs, then position over the lime curd. Top each pair of legs with an overturned cupcake so that the cupcake conceals the top parts of the legs. Serve.

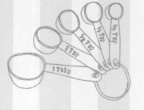

CHAPTER 5
HIDDEN
SURPRISES

Heart in a Cupcake

makes 12

280 g/10 oz plain flour

2¼ tsp baking powder

½ tsp salt

150 g/5½ oz unsalted butter, softened, plus extra for greasing

300 g/10½ oz caster sugar

1 tbsp vanilla extract

3 large eggs

175 ml/6 fl oz milk

pink food colouring

pink gum paste hearts, to decorate

frosting

3 large egg whites

175 g/6 oz granulated sugar

225 g/8 oz unsalted butter, softened

1 tsp vanilla extract

pink food colouring

1. Preheat the oven to 180°C/350°F/Gas Mark 4 and grease a 23-cm/9-inch round cake tin. Draw a straight line down the middle of the base (outside) of each of 12 paper cases. Place the cases in a 12-hole cupcake tin, with the lines all facing the same direction. Remember which direction the lines are facing because this is the direction in which you will place the hearts.

2. Sift together the flour, baking powder and salt in a bowl. Put the butter and caster sugar into a separate bowl and beat until pale and fluffy. Add the vanilla extract, then add the eggs, one at a time, beating after each addition. Add half of the flour mixture and the milk and beat until incorporated. Add the remaining flour mixture and mix.

3. Transfer about one third of the batter to a separate bowl and mix in several drops of pink food colouring until evenly incorporated. Spread the batter evenly in the prepared cake tin and bake in the preheated oven for 18 minutes, or until the cake is just cooked through. Leave to cool in the tin for 1–2 minutes, then turn out onto a wire rack and leave to cool completely (do not switch off the oven).

4. Use a 4-cm/1½-inch heart-shaped cutter to cut out 12 hearts from the pink cake. Discard the trimmings. Spoon a generous tablespoon of the remaining cake batter into the base of one of the paper cases and then stand a heart vertically in the middle, lining it up with the line drawn on the base of the case. Spoon more batter around the sides of the heart until the case is about two-thirds full. Repeat to fill all 12 cases. Cover the cupcake tin with foil to prevent the pre-baked hearts drying out.

5. Bake in the preheated oven for 20 minutes, until risen and golden. Leave to cool in the tin for 1-2 minutes, then transfer to a wire rack to cool completely.

6. To make the frosting, put the egg whites and granulated sugar in a heatproof bowl set over a saucepan of gently simmering water and whisk until the sugar has completely dissolved. Remove from the heat and whisk the mixture for 4-5 minutes, until it holds stiff peaks. Add the butter 2 tablespoons at a time, and continue to whisk until it holds stiff peaks. Add the vanilla extract and several drops of pink food colouring and beat until the colour is evenly incorporated. Gradually beat in more food colouring until the desired shade is achieved. Spoon the frosting into a piping bag fitted with a star-shaped tip.

7. Pipe the frosting onto the cupcakes and sprinkle with gum paste hearts. Cut in half to serve.

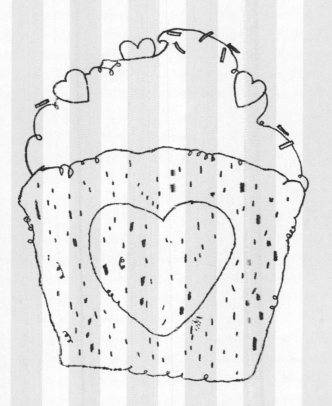

Chapter 5
Hidden Surprises

Top tip
Use the lines on the paper
cases as a guide when slicing
the cupcakes in half so that the
hearts will show.

Rainbow Cupcakes

makes 12

190 g/6¾ oz plain flour

1½ tsp baking powder

¼ tsp salt

55 g/2 oz unsalted butter, softened

55 g/2 oz vegetable shortening

200 g/7 oz caster sugar

2 tsp vanilla extract

4 large egg whites

125 ml/4 fl oz milk

red, yellow, green and blue food colourings

hundreds and thousands, to decorate

frosting

3 large egg whites

150 g/5½ oz granulated sugar

225 g/8 oz unsalted butter, softened

1 tsp vanilla extract

1. Preheat the oven to 180°C/350°F/Gas Mark 4 and line a 12-hole cupcake tin with paper cases.

2. Sift together the flour, baking powder and salt in a bowl. Put the butter, shortening and caster sugar into a separate bowl and beat until pale and fluffy. Add the vanilla extract, then add the egg whites, one at a time, beating after each addition. Add half of the flour mixture and the milk and beat until incorporated. Add the remaining flour mixture and mix.

3. Separate the batter into six small bowls. Colour one bowl of batter red using 8–10 drops of red food colouring. Colour one bowl orange with 8 drops of yellow food colouring and 4 drops of red food colouring. Colour one bowl yellow with 8 drops of yellow food colouring. Colour one bowl green with 8 drops of green food colouring. Colour one bowl blue with 8 drops of blue food colouring. Colour one bowl purple with 8 drops of red food colouring and 4 drops of blue food colouring. Beat each bowl of batter until the colour is evenly incorporated.

4. Spoon the batter into the paper cases one colour at a time, starting with purple. Drop a generous spoonful into each case, smoothing it out with the back of the spoon so that it covers the entire base. Then drop in a generous spoonful of blue batter, smoothing with the back of the spoon so that it covers all the purple batter. Continue with the green, yellow, orange and red batters. Bake in the preheated oven for 20 minutes, or until a cocktail stick inserted into the centre of a cupcake comes out clean. Leave to cool in the tin for 1–2 minutes, then transfer to a wire rack to cool completely.

5. To make the frosting, put the egg whites and granulated sugar in a heatproof bowl set over a saucepan of gently simmering water and whisk until the sugar has completely dissolved. Remove from the heat and whisk the mixture for 4–5 minutes, until it holds stiff peaks. Add the butter, 2 tablespoons at a time, and continue to whisk until it holds stiff peaks. Add the vanilla extract and beat until just combined. Spoon the frosting into a piping bag fitted with a star-shaped tip.

6. Pipe the frosting onto the cupcakes, sprinkle over the hundreds and thousands and serve.

Top tip

A marbled cake batter is just as effective and only needs 2 colours — red and plain cake batter is ideal for a faux red velvet cupcake.

3

4

6

Baby Shower Cupcakes

makes 12

190 g/6¾ oz plain flour

1½ tsp baking powder

¼ tsp salt

115 g/4 oz unsalted butter, softened

200 g/7 oz caster sugar

2 tsp vanilla extract

2 large eggs

125 ml/4 fl oz milk

pink or blue sprinkles, to decorate

icing toppers

white ready-to-roll fondant icing

pink or blue writing icing

custard filling

1 egg yolk

60 g/2¼ oz caster sugar

2 tbsp cornflour

225 ml/8 fl oz milk

pinch of salt

1 tsp vanilla extract

pink or blue food colouring

1. To make the icing toppers, knead the fondant icing until pliable. Roll out to 5 mm/¼ inch thick and cut out 12 rounds using a 2.5-cm/1-inch round biscuit cutter. Lay the rounds on a sheet of baking paper and use the writing icing to write on each topper. Set aside to dry.

2. Preheat the oven to 180°C/350°F/Gas Mark 4 and line a 12-hole cupcake tin with paper cases.

3. Sift together the flour, baking powder and salt in a bowl. Put the butter and caster sugar into a separate bowl and beat until pale and fluffy. Add the vanilla extract, then add the eggs, one at a time, beating after each addition. Add half of the flour mixture and the milk and beat until incorporated. Add the remaining flour mixture and mix.

4. Spoon the batter into the paper cases and bake in the preheated oven for 20 minutes, until risen and golden. Leave to cool in the tin for 1–2 minutes, then transfer to a wire rack to cool completely.

5. To make the custard filling, put the egg yolk in a large heatproof bowl and beat. Combine the caster sugar, cornflour, milk and salt in a saucepan and bring to the boil over a medium heat, stirring constantly. Boil, stirring, for 1 minute. Remove from the heat and stir 1 tablespoon of the milk mixture into the egg yolk, stirring constantly. Transfer the egg yolk to the milk mixture, stirring vigorously. Return to a low heat and stir constantly, until thickened. Stir in the vanilla extract and transfer the custard to a mixing bowl. Add pink or blue food colouring. Cover with clingfilm, pressing the clingfilm directly onto the surface of the custard and chill in the refrigerator until required.

frosting

115 g/4 oz unsalted butter, softened

about 250 g/7 oz icing sugar (see method)

2 tbsp milk

2 tsp vanilla extract

¼ tsp salt

6. To make the frosting, put the butter into a bowl and beat with an electric mixer until pale and creamy. Add the icing sugar, milk, vanilla extract and salt. Beat until well combined. Add more icing sugar, if necessary, to achieve a piping consistency.

7. Use an apple corer to remove the centre of each cupcake, reserving the 'core'. Spoon the filling into the holes, filling halfway. Cut the reserved cupcake 'cores' in half and discard 12 of the cake pieces. Place the remaining 'cores' on top of the custard. Using a palette knife spread an even layer of frosting on top of the cupcakes.

8. Spoon any remaining frosting into a piping bag fitted with a star-shaped tip. Pipe the frosting onto the cupcakes, then top with sprinkles and set the icing toppers on top. Serve.

4

5

7

Top tip

In the US, mums-to-be have cakes baked especially for their baby shower — with either blue or pink inside, to reveal the gender of the baby to guests.

Pinata Cupcakes

makes 12

125 g/4½ oz plain flour

60 g/2¼ oz cocoa powder

1½ tsp baking powder

¼ tsp salt

115 g/4 oz unsalted butter, softened

200 g/7 oz caster sugar

2 tsp vanilla extract

2 large eggs

125 ml/4 fl oz double cream

frosting

115 g/4 oz unsalted butter, softened

about 250 g/9 oz icing sugar (see method)

2 tbsp milk

1 tsp vanilla extract

pinch of salt

to decorate

350 g/12 oz plain chocolate-flavoured cake covering, broken into pieces

4½ tsps vegetable oil

450 g/1 lb mixed sweets

piping gel

hundreds and thousands

1. Preheat the oven to 180°C/350°F/Gas Mark 4 and line a 12-hole cupcake tin with paper cases.

2. Sift together the flour, cocoa powder, baking powder and salt in a bowl. Put the butter and caster sugar into a separate bowl and beat until pale and fluffy. Add the vanilla extract, then add the eggs, one at a time, beating after each addition. Add half of the flour mixture and the cream and beat until incorporated. Add the remaining flour mixture and mix.

3. Spoon the batter into the paper cases and bake in the preheated oven for 20 minutes, until risen and a cocktail stick inserted into the centre of a cupcake comes out clean. Leave to cool in the tin for 1–2 minutes, then transfer to a wire rack to cool completely.

4. To make the frosting, put the butter into a bowl and beat with an electric mixer until creamy. Add the icing sugar, milk, vanilla extract and salt and beat until well combined. Add more icing sugar, if necessary, to achieve a piping consistency.

5. Using a palette knife, spread the frosting evenly onto the cupcakes, making sure the frosting goes all the way to the edges of the paper cases.

6. To decorate, put the chocolate-flavoured cake covering and oil into a heatproof bowl set over a saucepan of gently simmering water and stir until the chocolate has completely melted. Spoon about 1 tablespoon of chocolate into a 7.5-cm/3-inch dome-shaped mould. Turn the mould slowly and use the back of a spoon to spread the chocolate in a thin layer, coating the entire cavity of the mould. Place the mould in the freezer for 5–10 minutes, or until the chocolate is set. Once set, carefully unmould the chocolate dome and store in the refrigerator until required. Repeat to make 12 chocolate domes.

7. Stand a dome upside-down on the work surface and fill it with a large spoonful of sweets. Place a frosted cupcake upside-down on top of the dome so that the frosting is pressed into the edge of the chocolate. Turn the cupcake right side up and set aside. Repeat until you have filled and assembled all 12 cupcakes. Using a small brush, brush the top of each dome with piping gel. Sprinkle with hundreds and thousands and leave to set. Serve.

Top tip

Use a plastic or silicone dome-shaped chocolate mould about 7.5 cm/ 3 inches in diameter to make the chocolate domes.

Ice Cream Cone Cupcakes

makes 12

190 g/6¾ oz plain flour

1½ tsp baking powder

¼ tsp salt

115 g/4 oz unsalted butter, softened

200 g/7 oz caster sugar

2 tsp vanilla extract

2 large eggs

125 ml/4 fl oz milk

85 g/3 oz plain chocolate chips

12 flat-bottom ice cream cones

hundreds and thousands, to decorate

frosting

115 g/4 oz unsalted butter, softened

about 250 g/9 oz icing sugar (see method)

1 tbsp milk

1 tsp vanilla extract

pinch of salt

1. Preheat the oven to 180°C/350°F/Gas Mark 4 and line a 12-hole cupcake tin with paper cases.

2. Sift together the flour, baking powder and salt in a bowl. Put the butter and caster sugar into a separate bowl and beat until pale and fluffy. Add the vanilla extract, then add the eggs, one at a time, beating after each addition. Add half of the flour mixture and the milk and beat until incorporated. Add the remaining flour mixture and mix. Stir in the chocolate chips.

3. Spoon the batter into the paper cases and then place an upside-down ice cream cone on top of the batter in each hole of the tin, gently pressing down the cone as far as it will go. Bake in the preheated oven for 20 minutes, or until a cocktail stick inserted into the cupcake batter comes out clean (the cones may tilt off to the side as the cupcakes rise). Leave to cool in the tin for 1–2 minutes, then transfer to a wire rack to cool completely.

4. To make the frosting, put the butter, icing sugar, milk, vanilla extract and salt into a bowl and beat until well combined. Add more icing sugar, if necessary, to achieve a piping consistency.

5. Remove the paper cases from the cupcakes and stand the cones the right way up. Use a palette knife to spread the frosting over the cupcake, swirling to resemble scoops of vanilla ice cream. To serve, sprinkle with hundreds and thousands.

Hi-hat Cupcakes

makes 12

125 g/4½ oz plain flour

60 g/2¼ oz cocoa powder

1½ tsp baking powder

¼ tsp salt

115 g/4 oz unsalted butter, softened

200 g/7 oz caster sugar

2 tsp vanilla extract

2 large eggs

125 ml/4 fl oz double cream

ready-made fondant icing flowers, to decorate

frosting

4 large egg whites

200 g/7 oz granulated sugar

¼ tsp cream of tartar

1 tsp vanilla extract

chocolate coating

225 g/8 oz plain chocolate-flavoured cake covering, broken into pieces

2 tbsp rapeseed oil or other vegetable oil

1. Preheat the oven to 180°C/350°F/Gas Mark 4 and line a 12-hole cupcake tin with paper cases.

2. Sift together the flour, cocoa powder, baking powder and salt in a bowl. Put the butter and caster sugar into a separate bowl and beat until pale and fluffy. Add the vanilla extract, then add the eggs, one at a time, beating after each addition. Add half of the flour mixture and the cream and beat until incorporated. Add the remaining flour mixture and mix.

3. Spoon the batter into the paper cases and bake in the preheated oven for 20 minutes, until risen and a cocktail stick inserted into the centre of a cupcake comes out clean. Leave to cool in the tin for 1–2 minutes, then transfer to a wire rack to cool completely.

4. To make the frosting, put the egg whites, granulated sugar and cream of tartar in a heatproof bowl set over a saucepan of gently simmering water and whisk until the sugar has completely dissolved. Remove from the heat and whisk the mixture for 4–5 minutes, until it holds stiff peaks. Add the vanilla extract and beat until just combined.

5. Spoon the frosting into a piping bag fitted with a star-shaped tip and pipe onto the cupcakes, creating a high peak. Chill the frosted cupcakes in the refrigerator for at least 15 minutes.

6. To make the chocolate coating, place the chocolate-flavoured cake covering and oil in a heatproof bowl set over a saucepan of gently simmering water and stir until the chocolate has melted. Dip the chilled cupcakes into the chocolate so that the frosting is covered. Attach the fondant flowers and leave to set.

Top tip

For added fun-factor, add a vibrant
food colouring to the frosting, along
with the vanilla extract, and pipe
as instructed.

Baked-in Biscuit Cupcakes

makes 12

12 chocolate sandwich biscuits

125 g/4½ oz plain flour

60 g/2¼ oz cocoa powder

1½ tsp baking powder

¼ tsp salt

55 g/2 oz unsalted butter, softened

200 g/7 oz caster sugar

2 tsp vanilla extract

2 large eggs

125 ml/4 fl oz double cream

12 mini chocolate sandwich biscuits, to decorate

frosting

225 g/8 oz unsalted butter, softened

about 175 g/6 oz icing sugar (see method)

2 tbsp milk

1 tsp vanilla extract

pinch of salt

6 chocolate sandwich biscuits

1. Preheat the oven to 180°C/350°F/Gas Mark 4 and line a 12-hole cupcake tin with paper cases. Place a biscuit in the base of each case.

2. Sift together the flour, cocoa powder, baking powder and salt in a bowl. Put the butter and caster sugar into a separate bowl and beat until pale and fluffy. Add the vanilla extract, then add the eggs, one at a time, beating after each addition. Add half of the flour mixture and the cream and beat until incorporated. Add the remaining flour mixture and mix.

3. Spoon the batter into the paper cases over the biscuits and bake in the preheated oven for 20 minutes, until risen and a cocktail stick inserted into the centre of a cupcake comes out clean. Leave to cool in the tin for 1–2 minutes, then transfer to a wire rack to cool completely.

4. To make the frosting, put the butter into a bowl and beat with an electric mixer until creamy. Add the icing sugar, milk, vanilla extract and salt. Separate the 6 sandwich biscuits and scrape the cream filling into the frosting, reserving the biscuits. Beat together until well combined. Add more icing sugar, if necessary, to achieve a piping consistency.

5. In a food processor, coarsely grind the reserved biscuits. Add to the frosting and mix until just combined. Spoon the frosting into a piping bag fitted with a star-shaped tip and pipe onto the cupcakes. Decorate each cupcake with one of the mini biscuits and serve.

Funfetti Cupcakes

makes 12

190 g/6¾ oz plain flour

1½ tsp baking powder

¼ tsp salt

55 g/2 oz unsalted butter, softened

55 g/2 oz vegetable shortening

125 g/4½ oz caster sugar

2 tsp vanilla extract

4 large egg whites

125 ml/4 fl oz milk

75 g/2¾ oz hundreds and thousands

frosting

2 large egg whites

100 g/3½ oz granulated sugar

160 g/5¾ oz unsalted butter, softened

2 tsp vanilla extract

1. Preheat the oven to 180°C/350°F/Gas Mark 4 and line a 12-hole cupcake tin with paper cases.

2. Sift together the flour, baking powder and salt in a bowl. Put the butter, shortening and caster sugar into a separate bowl and beat until pale and fluffy. Add the vanilla extract, then add the egg whites, one at a time, beating between each addition. Add half of the flour mixture and the milk and beat until incorporated. Add the remaining flour mixture and mix. Stir in two thirds of the hundreds and thousands.

3. Spoon the batter into the paper cases and bake in the preheated oven for 20 minutes, until risen and golden. Leave to cool in the tin for 1–2 minutes, then transfer to a wire rack to cool completely.

4. To make the frosting, put the egg whites and granulated sugar in a heatproof bowl set over a saucepan of gently simmering water and whisk until the sugar has completely dissolved. Remove from the heat and whisk for 4–5 minutes. Add the butter, 2 tablespoons at a time, and continue to whisk until it holds stiff peaks. Add the vanilla extract and beat until just combined. Spoon the frosting into a piping bag fitted with a star-shaped tip.

5. Pipe the frosting onto the cupcakes and sprinkle over the remaining hundreds and thousands. Serve.

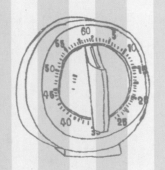

3

5

5

Pie in a Cupcake

makes 12

190 g/6¾ oz plain flour

1½ tsp baking powder

1 tsp ground cinnamon

¼ tsp salt

115 g/4 oz unsalted butter, softened

200 g/7 oz caster sugar

1 tsp vanilla extract

2 large eggs

125 ml/4 fl oz milk

mini pies

butter, for greasing

500 g/1 lb 2 oz fresh blueberries

1½ tsp finely grated lemon rind

1 tbsp lemon juice

3 tbsp plain flour, plus extra for dusting

75 g/2¾ oz caster sugar

200 g/7 oz ready-made shortcrust pastry, at room temperature

frosting

115 g/4 oz unsalted butter, softened

about 250 g/9 oz icing sugar (see method)

1 tbsp milk

1 tsp vanilla extract

1 tsp ground cinnamon

pinch of salt

yellow and brown food colourings

1. Preheat the oven to 190°C/375°F/Gas Mark 5. Grease a mini cupcake tin and line a 12-hole cupcake tin with paper cases.

2. To make the mini pies, put the blueberries, lemon rind, lemon juice, flour and caster sugar into a bowl and mix. Set aside.

3. Roll out the pastry on a lightly floured work surface and use a 7.5-cm/3-inch round cutter to cut out 12 rounds. Gather up and wrap the leftover pastry in clingfilm and set aside. Fit the rounds into the wells of the prepared mini muffin tin, pressing them down into the holes. Fill each round with a generous spoonful of the blueberry mixture, reserving the remainder.

4. Roll out the remaining pastry and use a 5-cm/2-inch round cutter to cut out 12 rounds for the tops of the mini pies. Place the rounds on top of the pies, crimping the edges together. Use a cocktail stick to pierce 2 holes in the top of each pie. Bake in the preheated oven for 20–25 minutes, or until golden brown and crisp. Remove from the oven (leave the oven on, but reduce the oven temperature to 180°C/350°F/Gas Mark 4), leave to cool in the tin for 3–5 minutes, then transfer to a wire rack to cool completely.

5. Put the reserved blueberry mixture into a small saucepan and stir in 4 tablespoons of water. Bring to the boil, then reduce the heat to low and simmer for about 5 minutes, or until the mixture thickens to a syrup. Using a food processor or hand blender, process the berry mixture to a chunky purée. Set aside to cool.

6. Sift together the flour, baking powder, cinnamon and salt in a bowl. Put the butter and caster sugar into a separate bowl and beat until pale and fluffy. Add the vanilla extract, then add the eggs, one at a time, beating after each addition. Add half of the flour mixture and the milk and beat until incorporated. Add the remaining flour mixture and mix.

7. Spoon 1 tablespoon of batter into each paper case. Place a mini pie in each case, nestling it into the batter. Spoon the remaining batter on top of the pies, making sure they are completely covered. Bake in the oven for 22–24 minutes, until risen and golden. Leave to cool in the tin for 1–2 minutes, then transfer to a wire rack to cool completely.

8. To make the frosting, put the butter, icing sugar, milk, vanilla extract, cinnamon and salt into a bowl and beat with an electric mixer until well combined. Add more icing sugar, if necessary, to achieve a piping consistency. Add a few drops of yellow food colouring and 1 drop of brown food colouring, and beat until evenly incorporated. Add more of both colours until a golden pastry colour is achieved. Spoon the frosting into a piping bag fitted with a flat 5-mm/¼-inch wide tip.

9. When the cupcakes have cooled, spread each one with 1 tablespoon of the puréed blueberry mixture, using the back of the spoon to spread the purée in an even layer that goes almost all the way to the edge of the cupcake. Pipe 2 parallel lines of frosting across the top of each cupcake and then 2 lines perpendicular to those to create a latticed effect. Pipe frosting around the edge of each cupcake, using a backwards and forwards motion to make it look like the pleated edge of a pie. Serve.

2

7

9

9

Top tip

Make the mini pies ahead of time and store them in the freezer for up to 1 month. Bring to room temperature before baking into the cupcakes.

S'mores Cupcakes

makes 12

125 g/4½ oz plain flour

85 g/3 oz cocoa powder, plus extra to decorate

1½ tsp baking powder

¼ tsp salt

115 g/4 oz unsalted butter, softened

200 g/7 oz caster sugar

2 tsp vanilla extract

2 large eggs

125 ml/4 fl oz double cream

40 g/1½ oz plain chocolate chips

biscuit base

115 g/4 oz digestive biscuits

125 g/4½ oz caster sugar

115 g/4 oz unsalted butter, melted

frosting

4 large egg whites

200 g/7 oz granulated sugar

¼ tsp cream of tartar

1 tsp vanilla extract

1. Preheat the oven to 180°C/350°F/Gas Mark 4 and line a 12-hole cupcake tin with paper cases.

2. To make the biscuit base, process all the ingredients in a food processor to make coarse crumbs. Spoon 1 tablespoon of the biscuit mixture into each paper case and flatten using the back of the spoon. Reserve any remaining mixture. Bake in the preheated oven for about 8 minutes, until golden brown (do not switch off the oven).

3. Sift together the flour, cocoa powder, baking powder and salt in a bowl. Put the butter and caster sugar into a separate bowl and beat with an electric mixer until pale and fluffy. Add the vanilla extract, then add the eggs, one at a time, beating after each addition. Add half of the flour mixture and the cream and beat until incorporated. Add the remaining flour mixture and mix. Stir in the chocolate chips.

4. Spoon the batter into the paper cases on top of the biscuit base and sprinkle the reserved crumb mixture over the top. Bake in the preheated oven for 20 minutes, or until a cocktail stick inserted into the centre of a cupcake comes out clean. Leave to cool in the tin for 1–2 minutes, then transfer to a wire rack to cool completely.

5. To make the frosting, put the egg whites, sugar and cream of tartar in a heatproof bowl set over a saucepan of gently simmering water and whisk until the sugar has completely dissolved. Remove from the heat and whisk for 4–5 minutes, until it holds stiff peaks. Add the vanilla extract and beat until just combined. Spoon the frosting into a piping bag fitted with a star-shaped tip and pipe the frosting onto the cupcakes. Dust with cocoa powder and serve.

Hidden Surprises
Chapter 5

Egg Cupcakes

makes 12

12 large eggs

190 g/6¾ oz plain flour

1½ tsp baking powder

¼ tsp salt

115 g/4 oz unsalted butter, softened

200 g/7 oz caster sugar

2 tsp vanilla extract

finely grated rind and juice of 1 lemon

125 ml/4 fl oz milk

to decorate

225 g/8 oz white chocolate-flavoured cake covering, broken into pieces

1 tbsp vegetable oil

piping gel

hundreds and thousands

1. To prepare the eggshells, poke a hole in the top of each egg using a chopstick. Using your fingers, gently break the shell to enlarge the hole until it is about 1 cm/½ inch across. Empty out the egg into a bowl. Repeat with another egg, then cover the bowl and refrigerate (they will be used in the cupcake batter). Empty the remaining eggs into a separate bowl, cover and store in the refrigerator.

2. Rinse the eggshells inside and out, under cold running water, then place them, hole side down, on a clean tea towel and leave to dry.

3. Preheat the oven to 180°C/350°F/Gas Mark 4.

4. Sift together the flour, baking powder and salt in a bowl. Put the butter and caster sugar into a separate bowl and beat until pale and fluffy. Add the vanilla extract, then add the 2 reserved eggs, one at a time, beating after each addition, until combined. Add the lemon rind and juice and half of the flour mixture and beat until incorporated. Add the milk and beat until incorporated. Add the remaining flour mixture and mix.

5. Transfer the batter to a piping bag fitted with a round tip (make sure the tip will fit into the openings in the eggshells). Carefully pipe batter into the eggshells, filling each just over half full. Place the eggs in a 12-hole cupcake tin, leaning them against the sides of the holes so that they stand up straight. If necessary, use crumpled foil to keep the eggs upright.

6. Bake in the preheated oven for 20 minutes, or until a cocktail stick inserted into the centre of an egg comes out clean. Leave to cool in the tin for 1–2 minutes, then transfer to a wire rack to cool completely. If the cake has risen out of the eggs, simply scrape off the surplus with a knife and discard.

7. Once cool enough to handle, peel the eggshells off the cupcakes and discard.

8. To decorate, put the chocolate-flavoured cake covering and oil into in a heatproof bowl set over a saucepan of gently simmering water and stir until the chocolate has completely melted. Dip the eggs into the chocolate, coating each egg halfway. Allow the excess chocolate to drip off into the bowl and then stand the eggs up, undipped side down, in a cupcake tin. If necessary use crumpled foil to keep the eggs upright. Repeat until all 12 cakes are half dipped, then chill in the refrigerator for 10–15 minutes, until the chocolate is set. If necessary, reheat the unused chocolate coating, then dip the other halves of the eggs and replace in the cupcake tin holes, with the set chocolate side downwards. Chill in the refrigerator for 10–15 minutes, until the chocolate is set.

9. Using a small brush, use the piping gel to paint shapes onto the eggs, then sprinkle with hundreds and thousands. Serve.

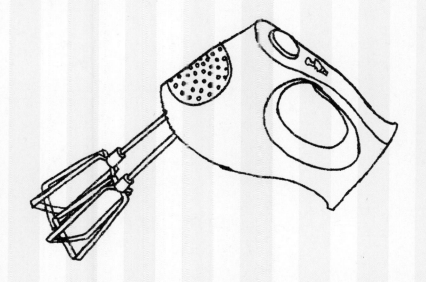

1

7

8

Top tip
You'll use 2 of the eggs for the cake batter. The 10 remaining eggs can be kept in the refrigerator, covered, for 2–3 days.

Index